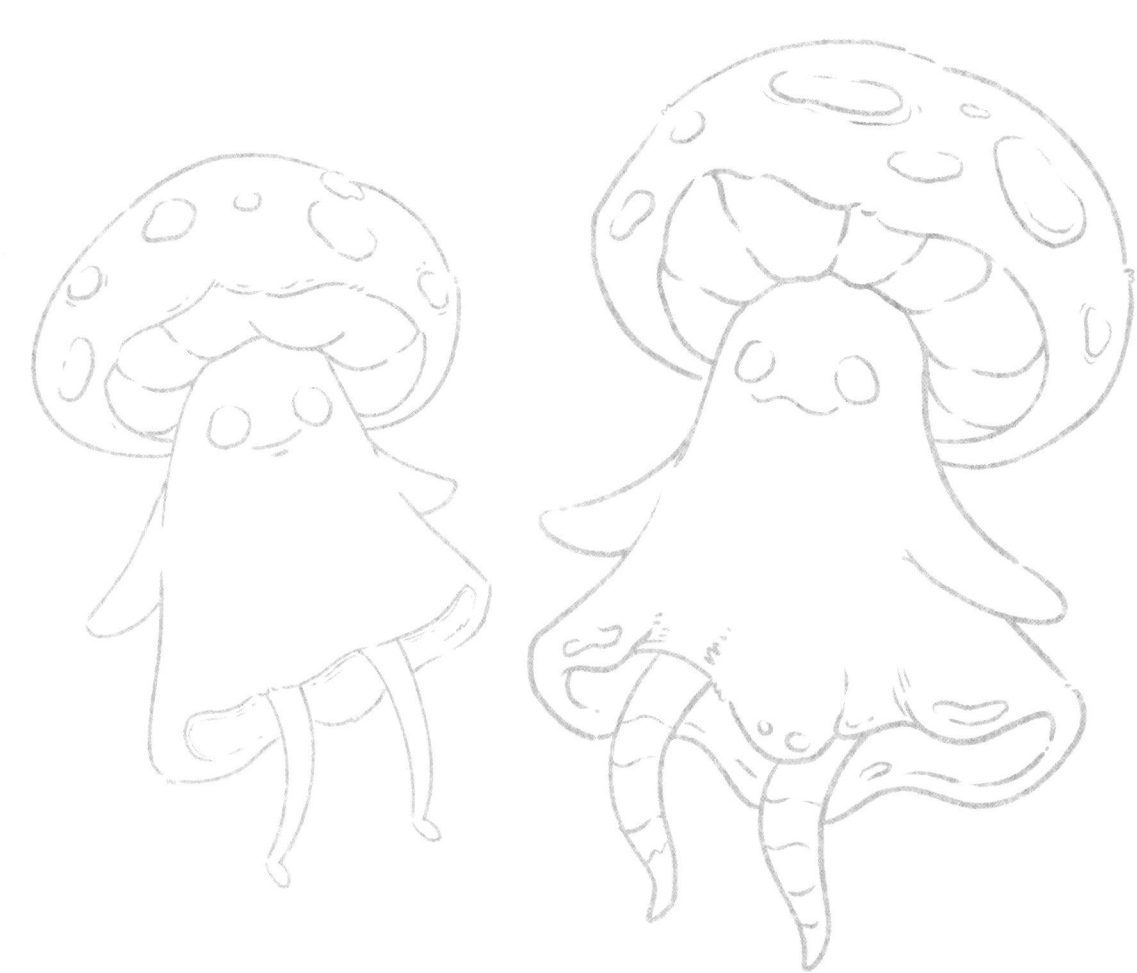

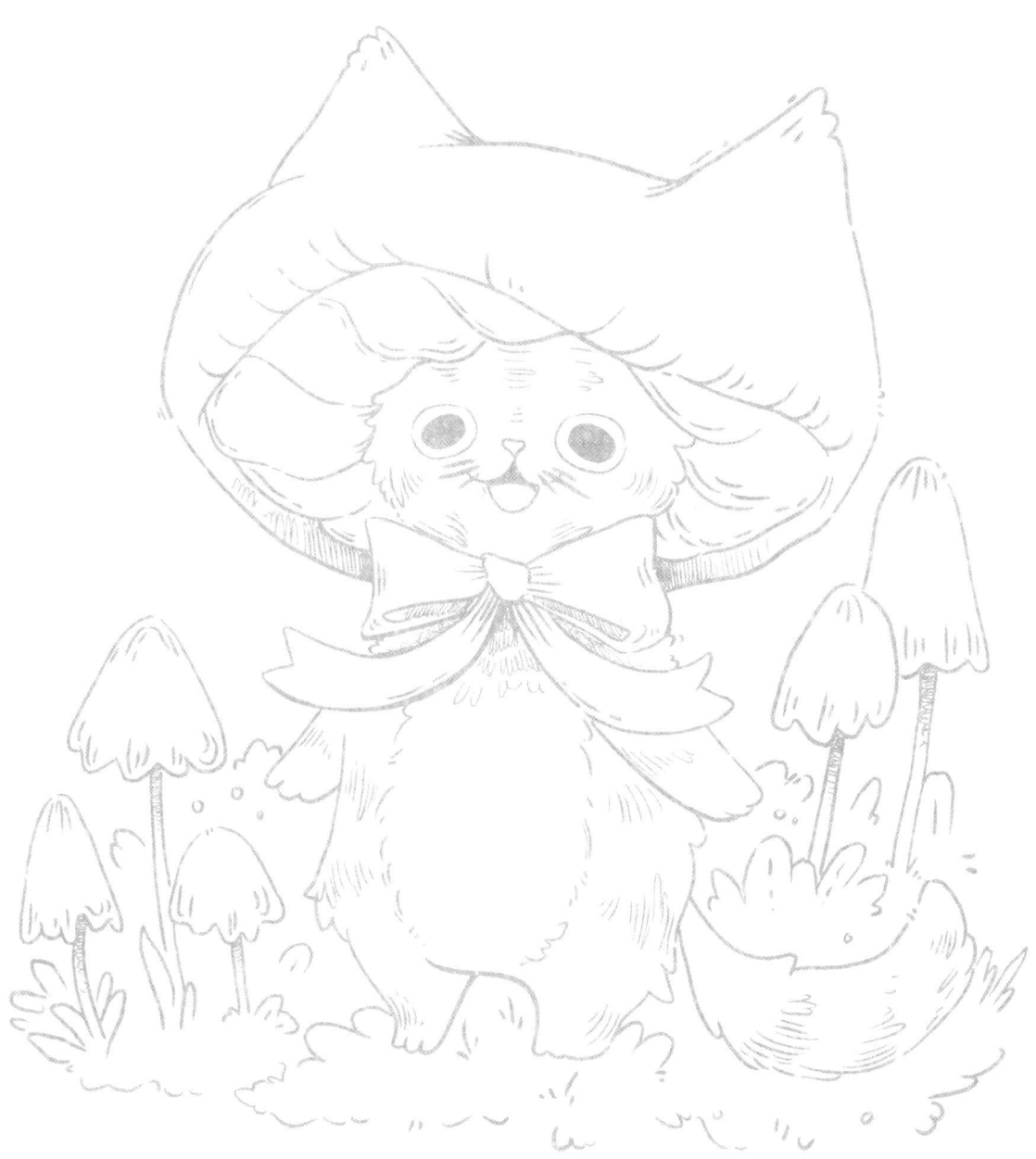

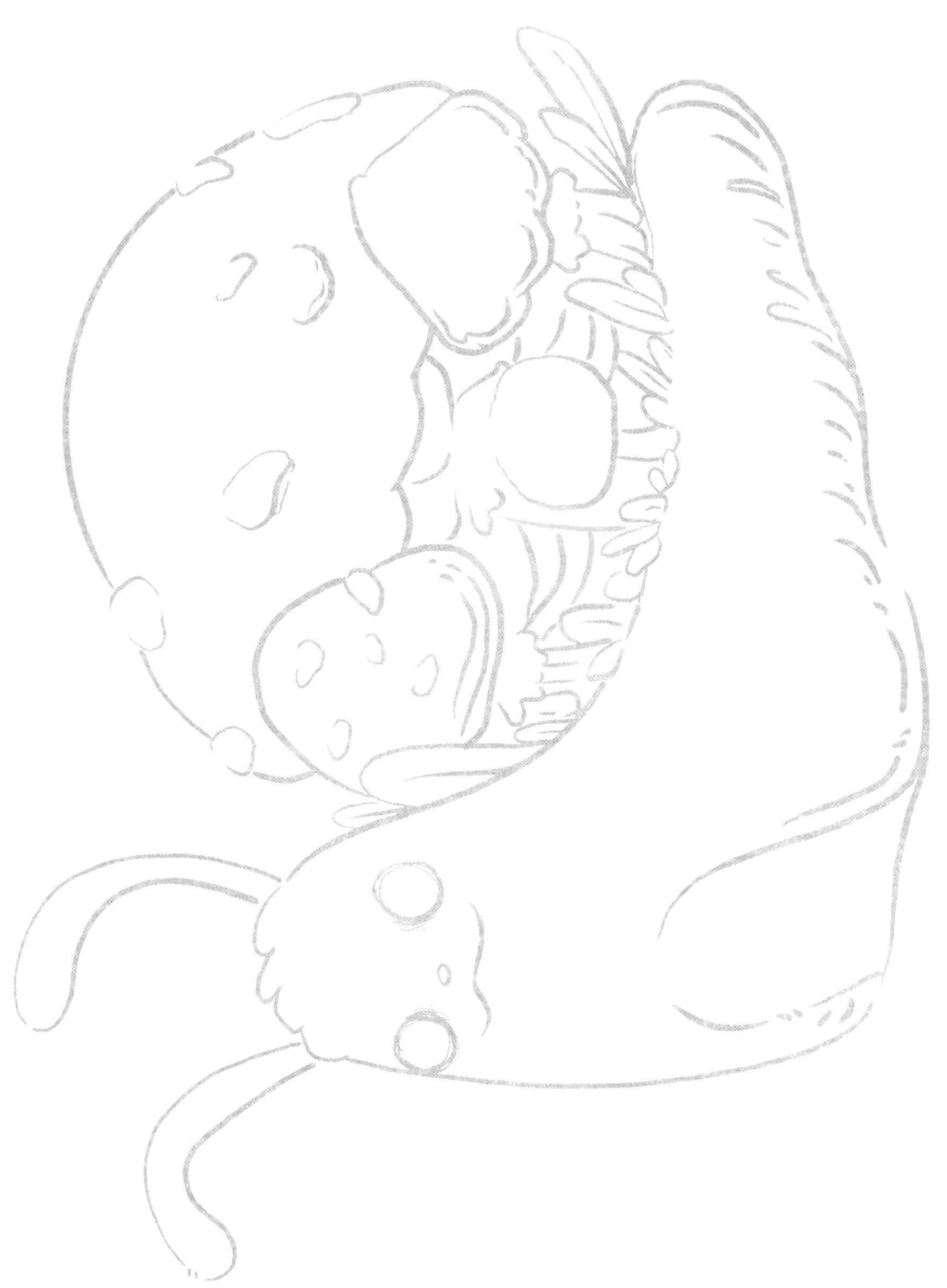

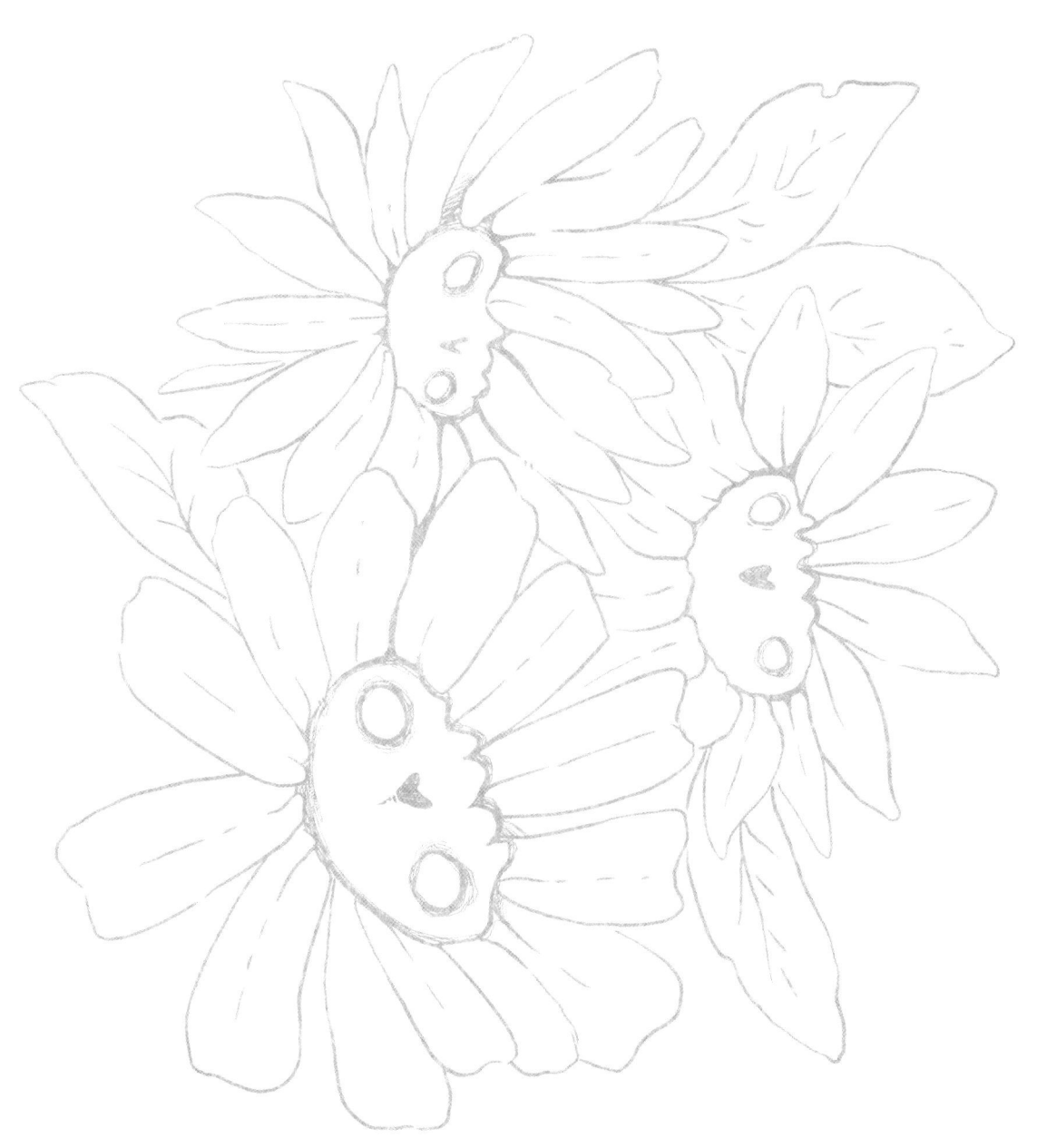

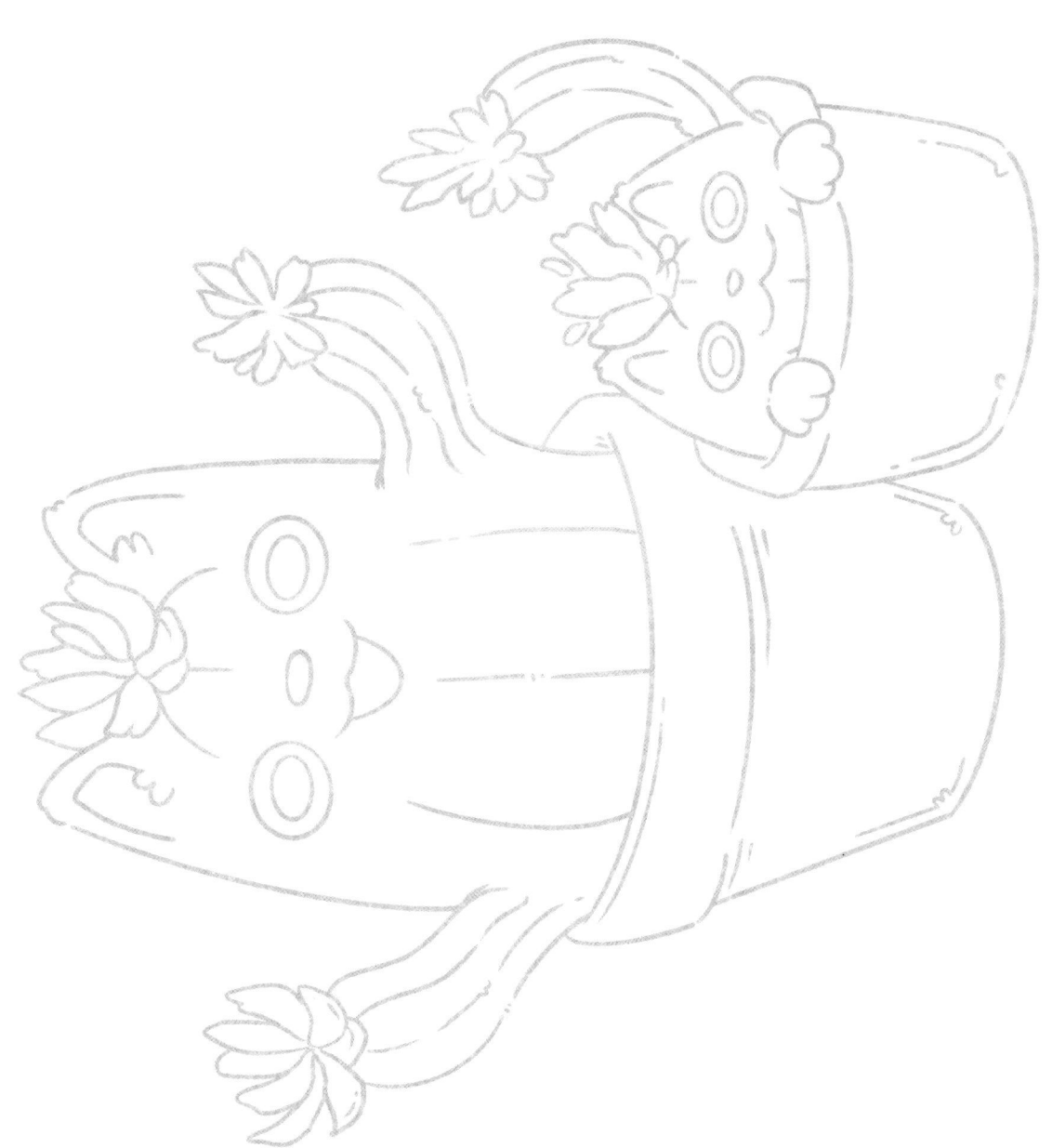

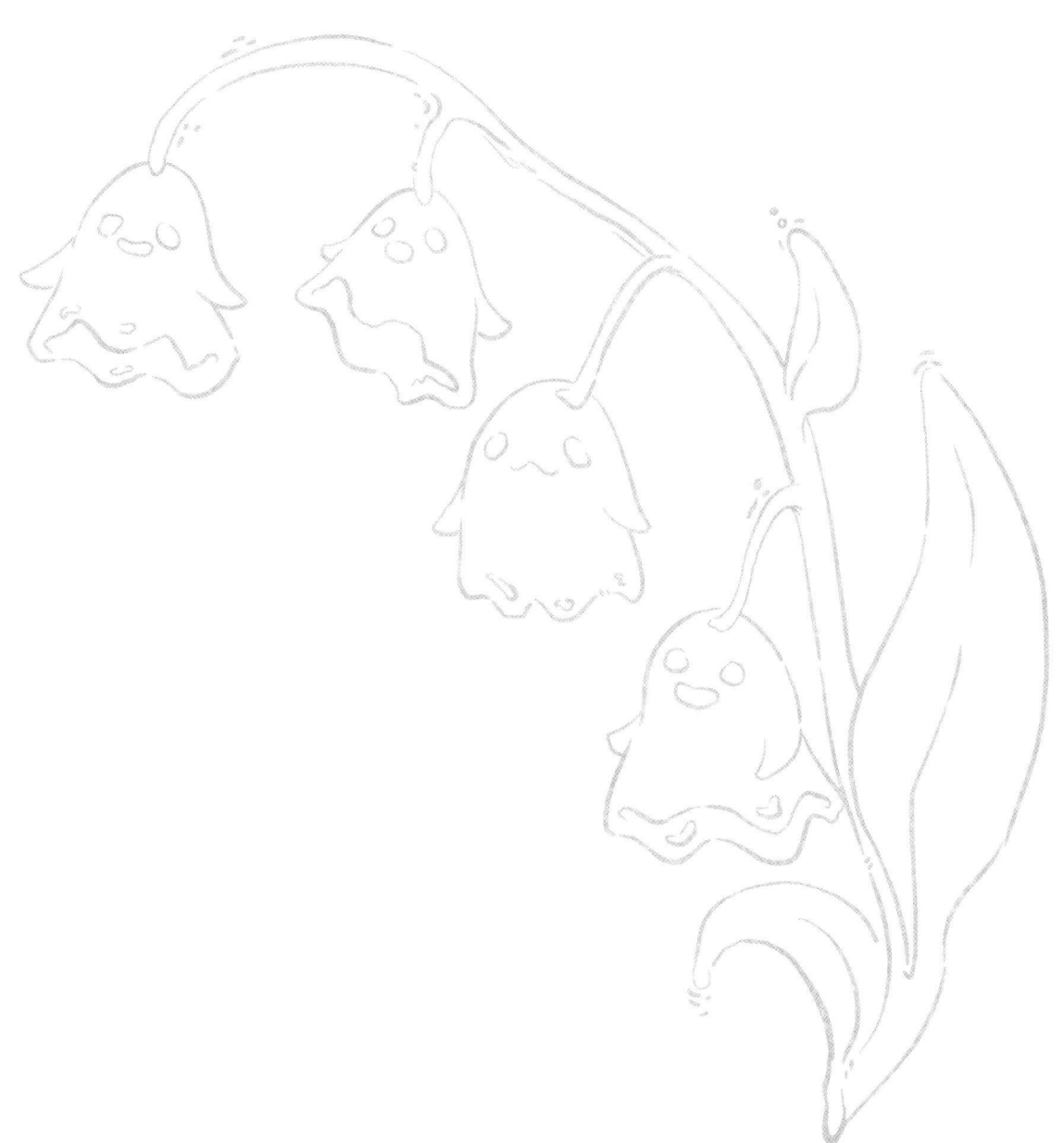

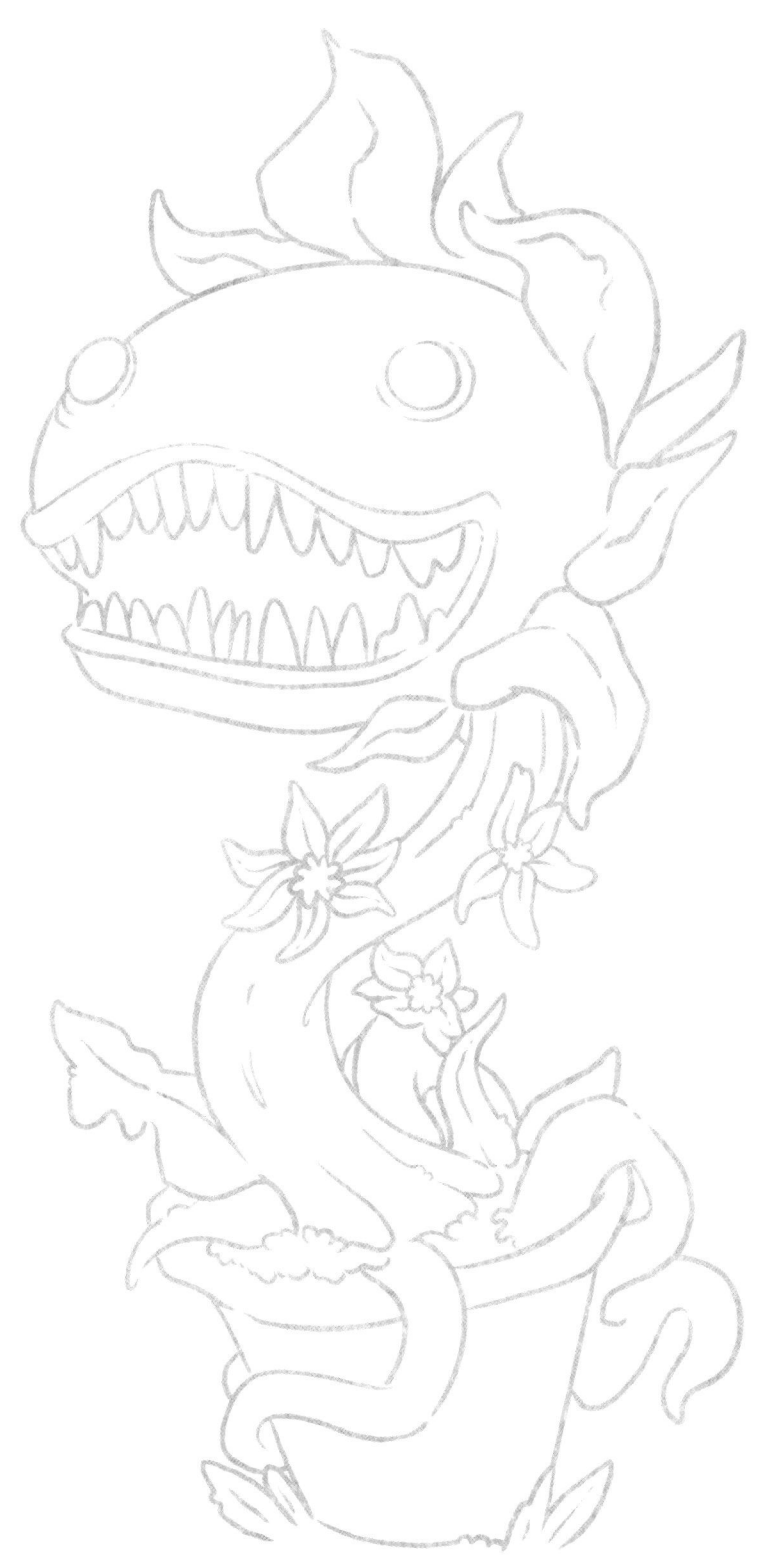

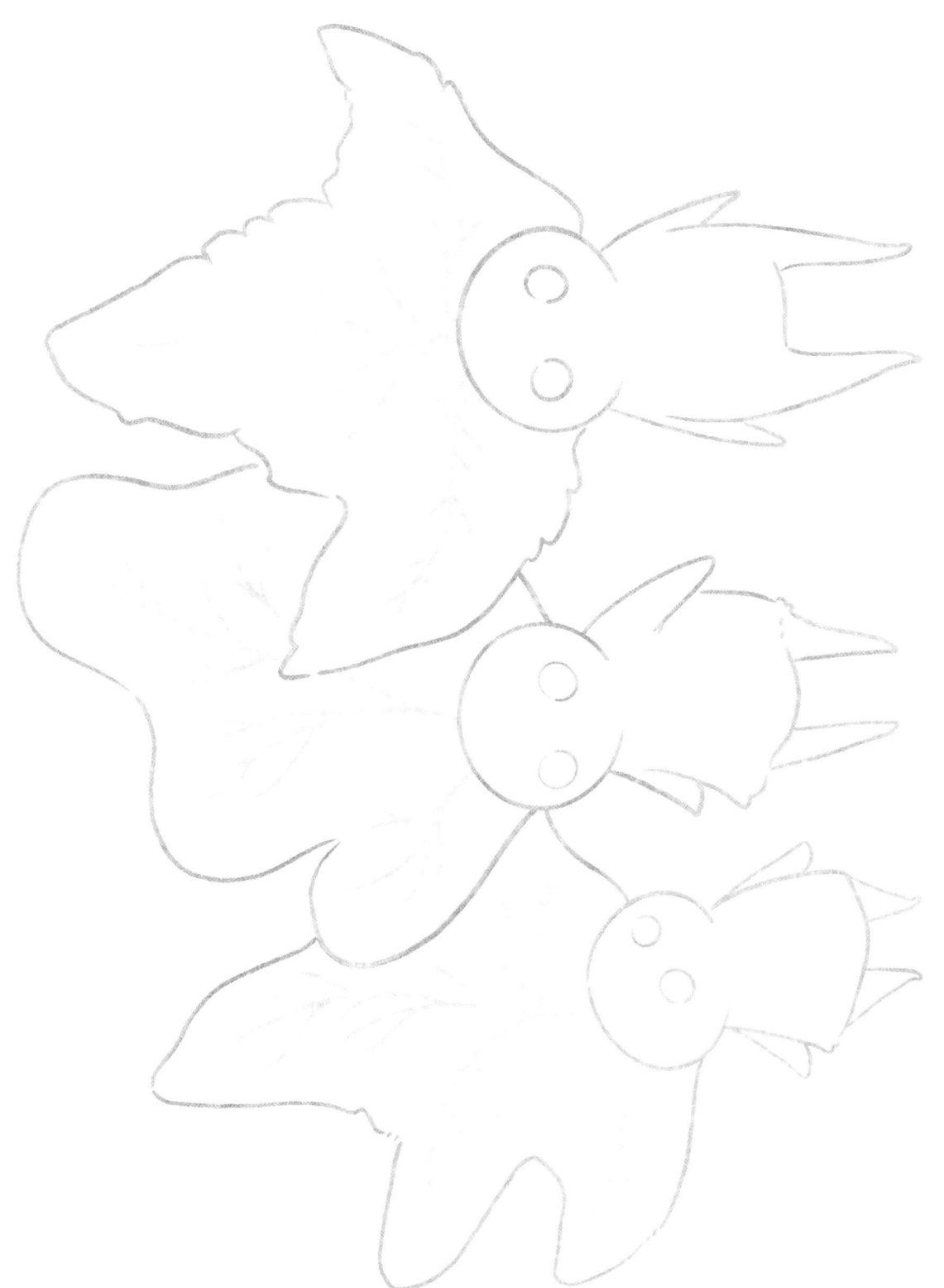

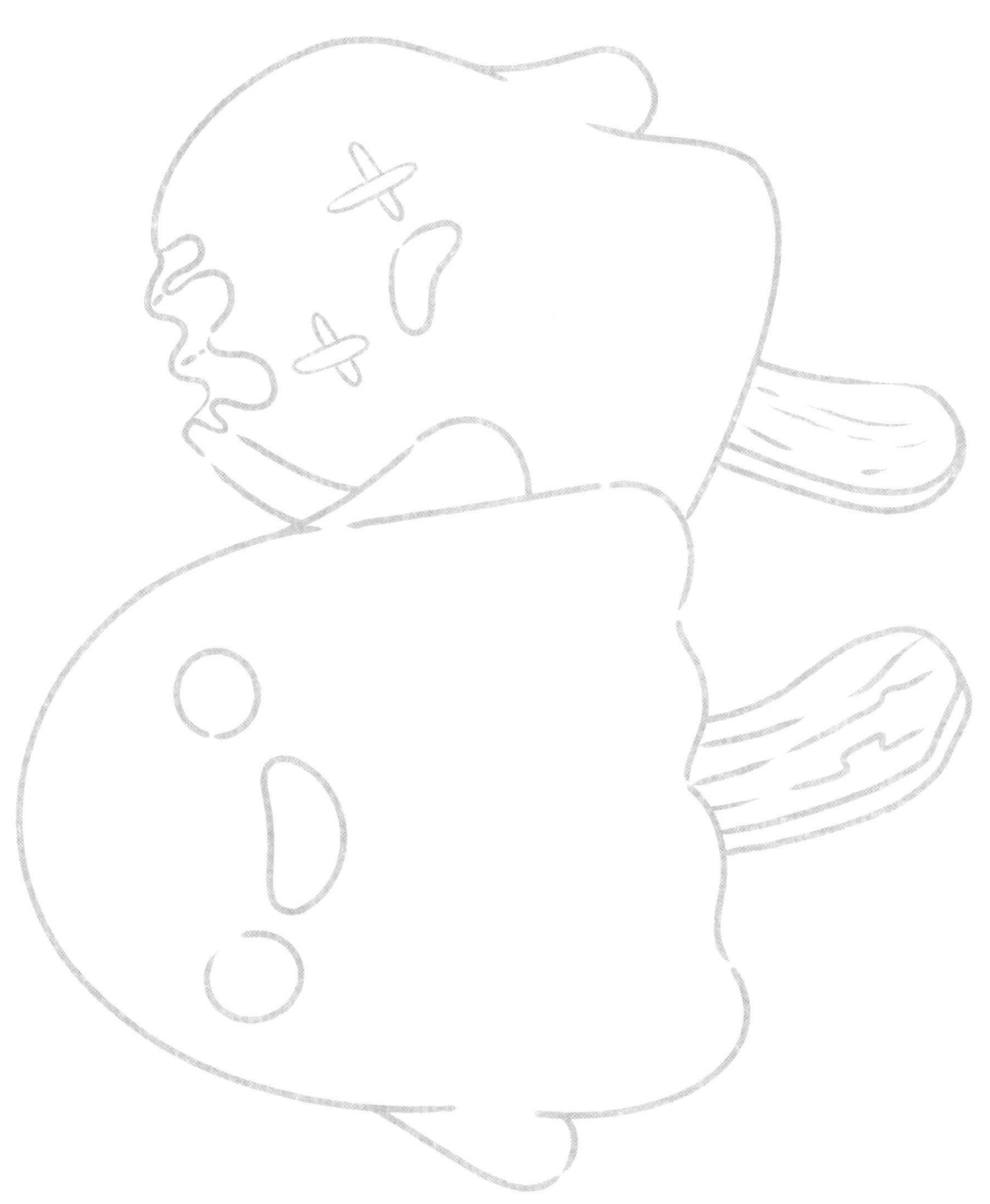

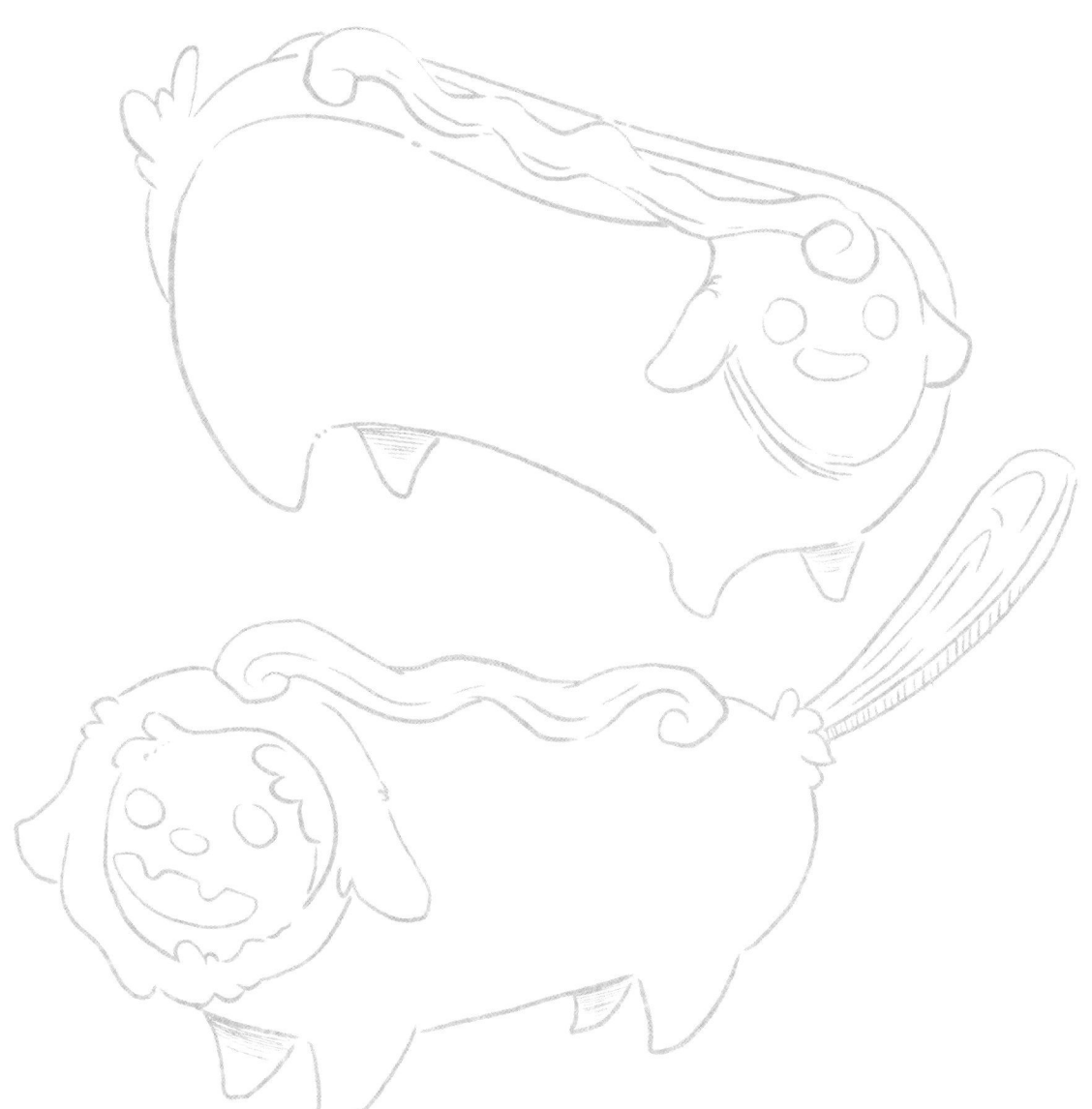

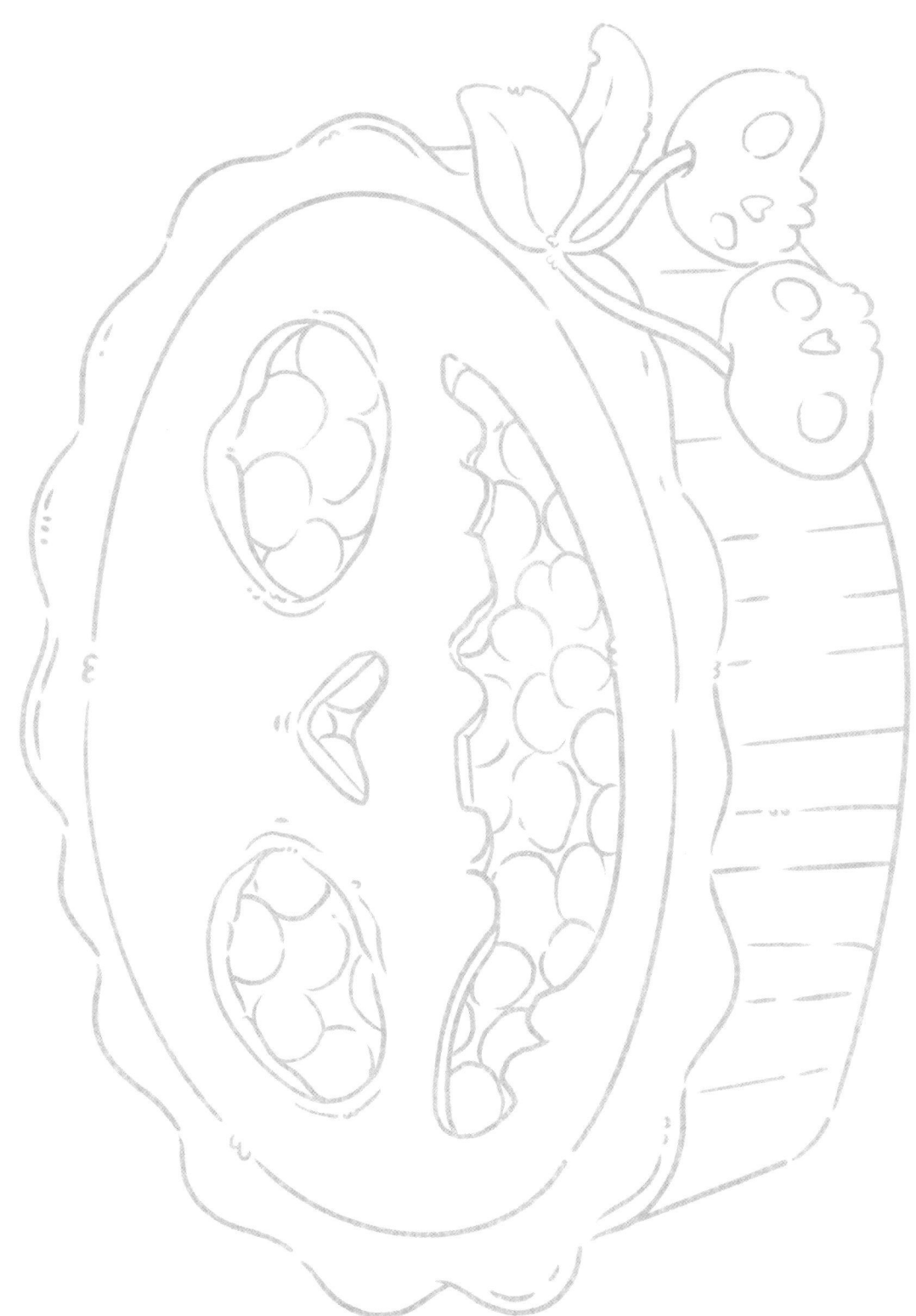

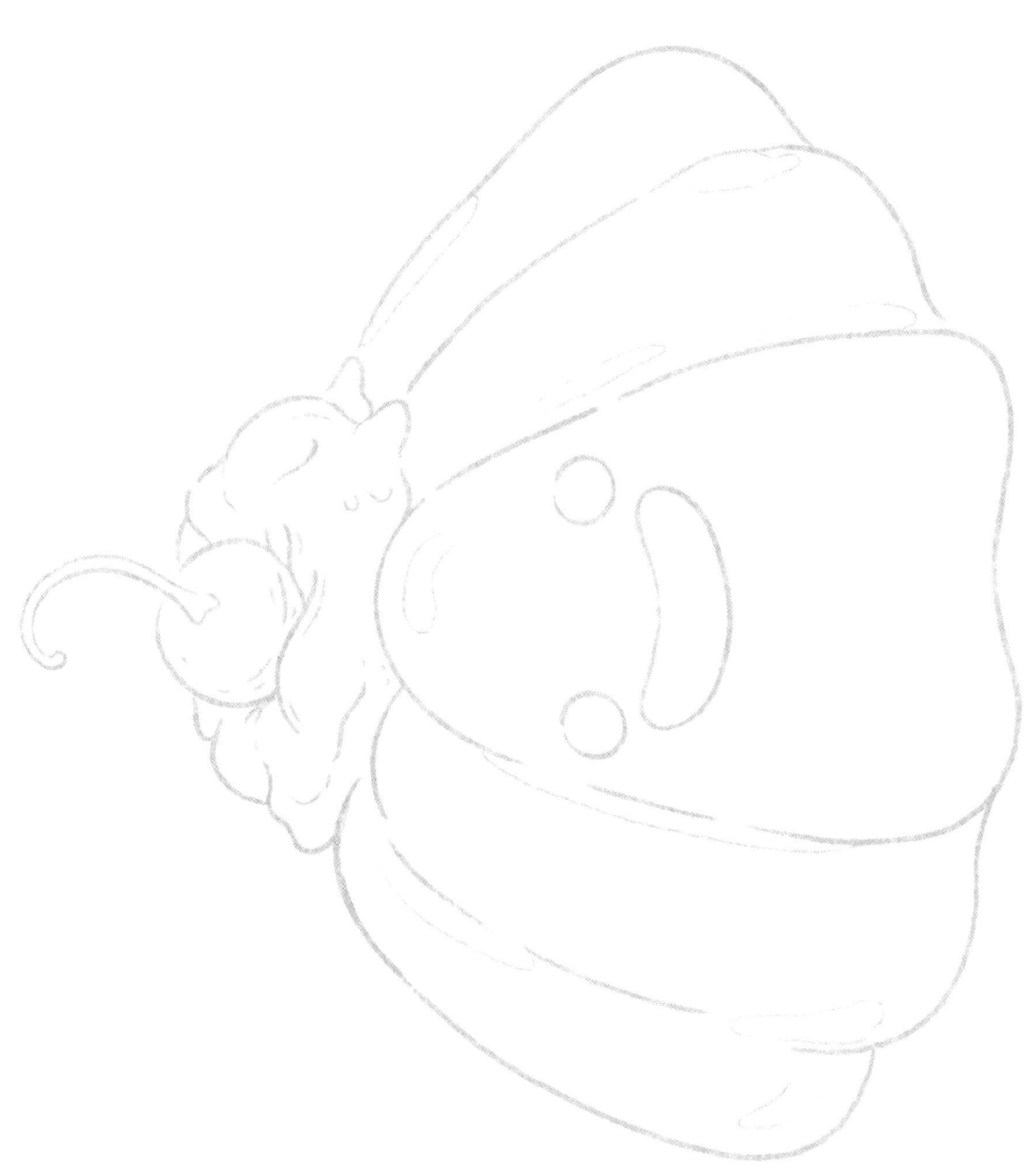

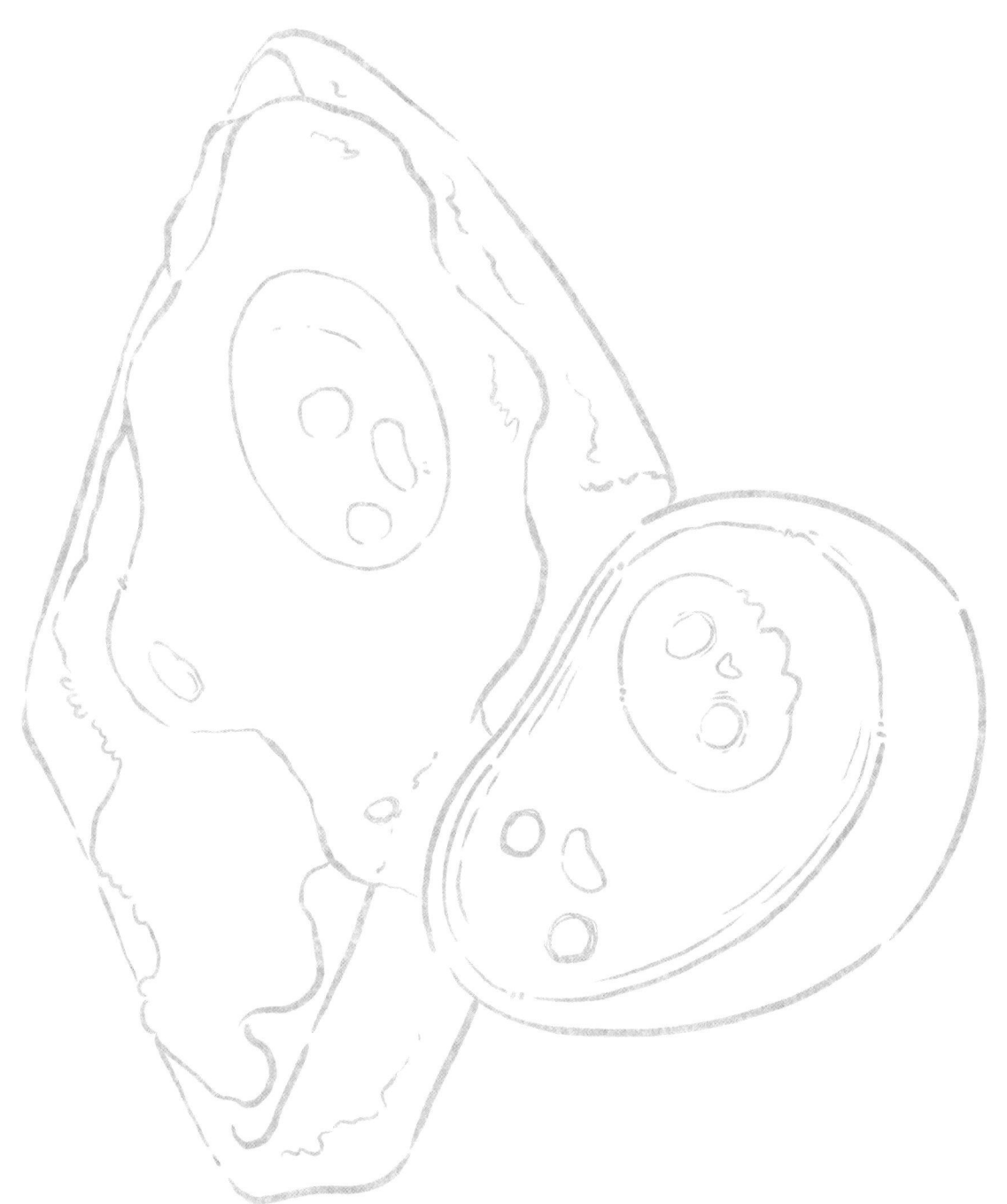

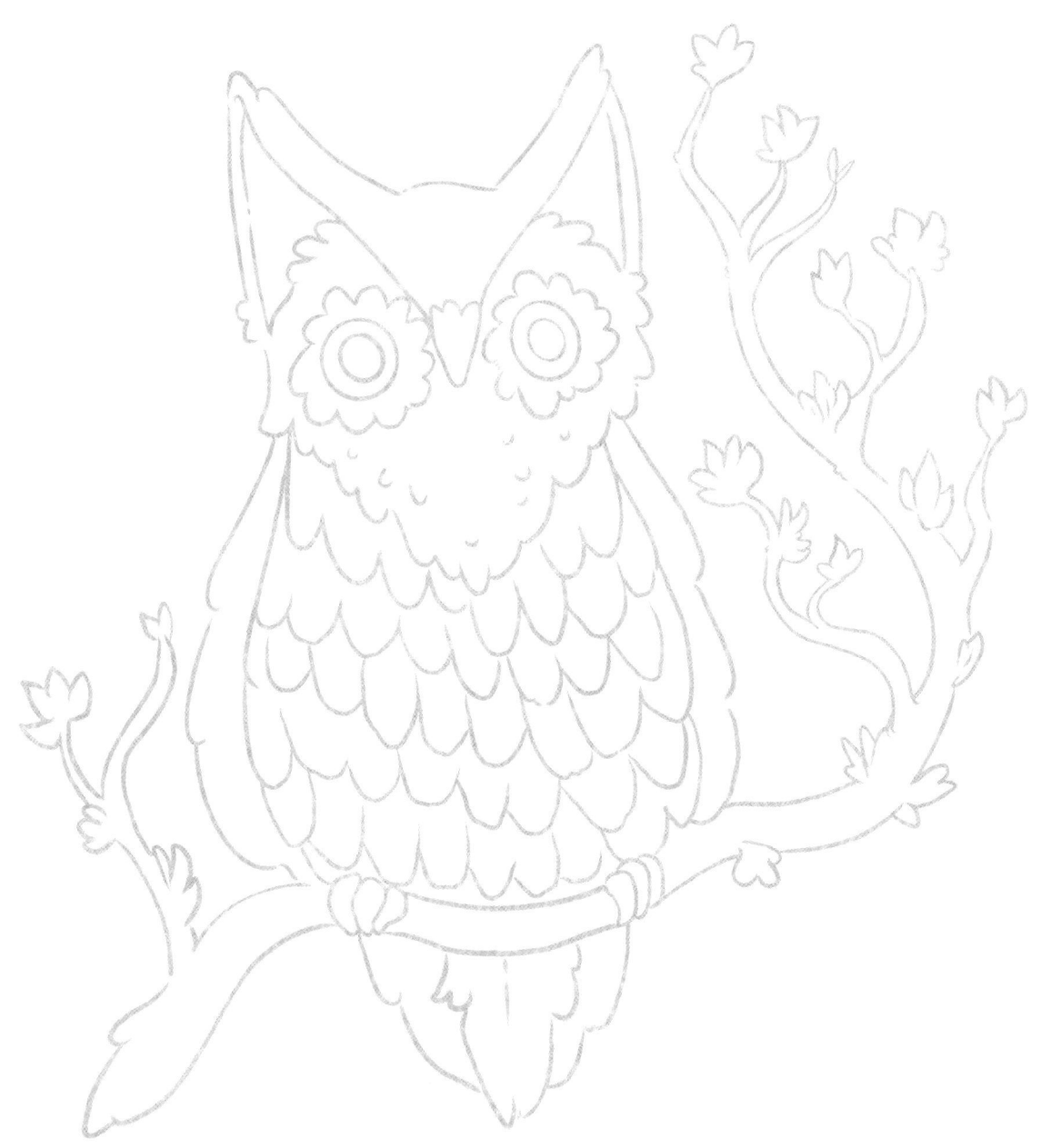

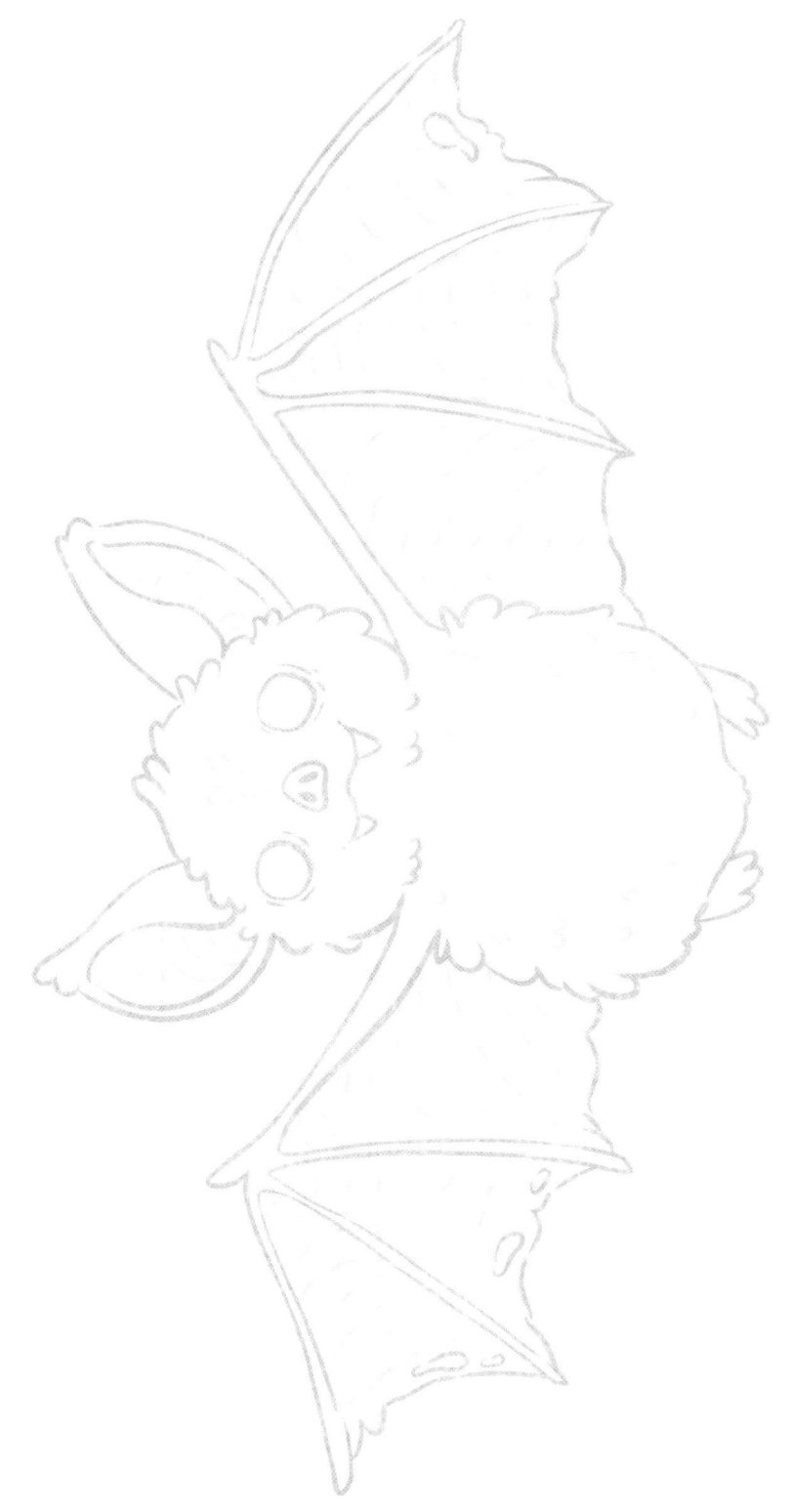

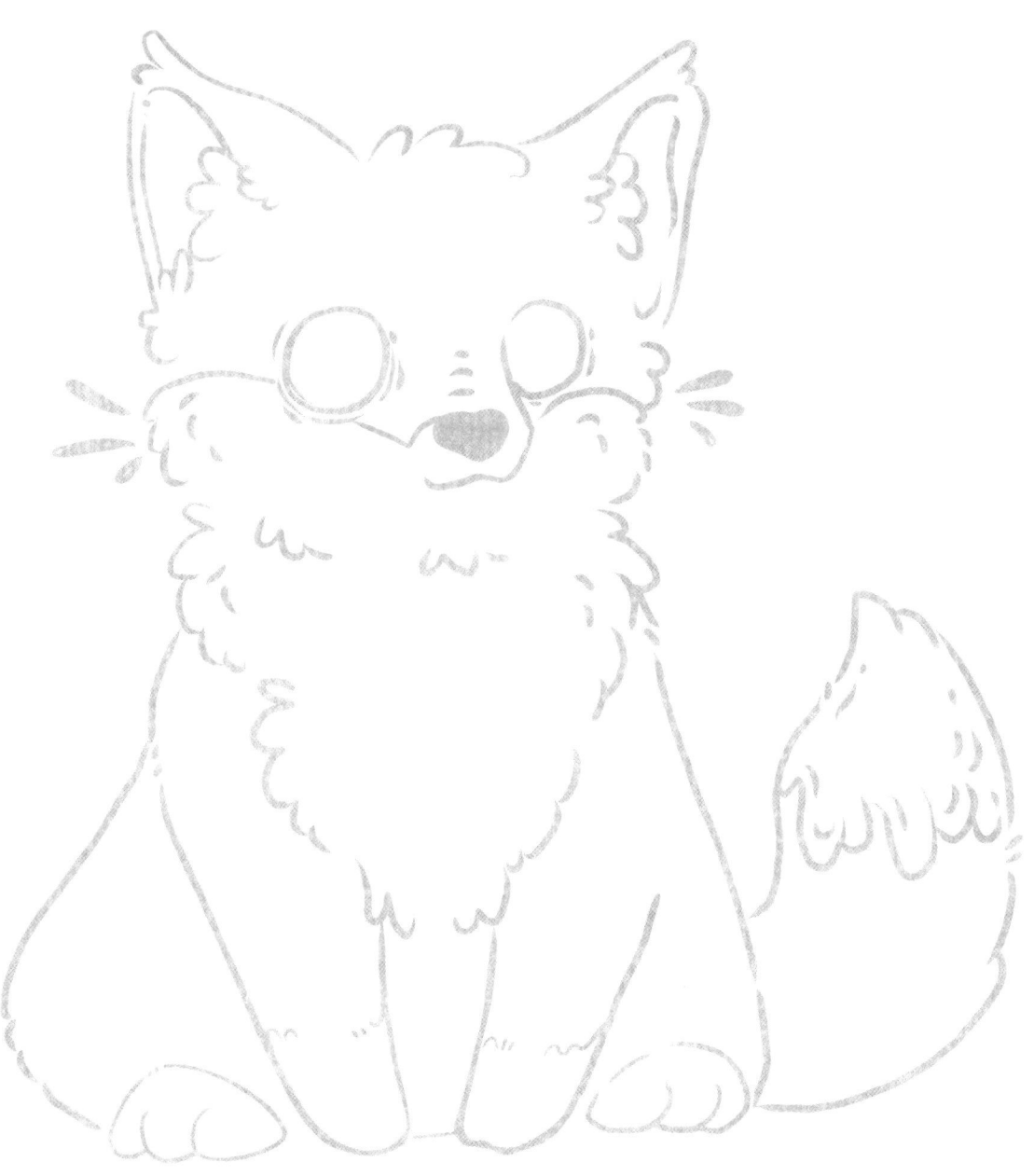

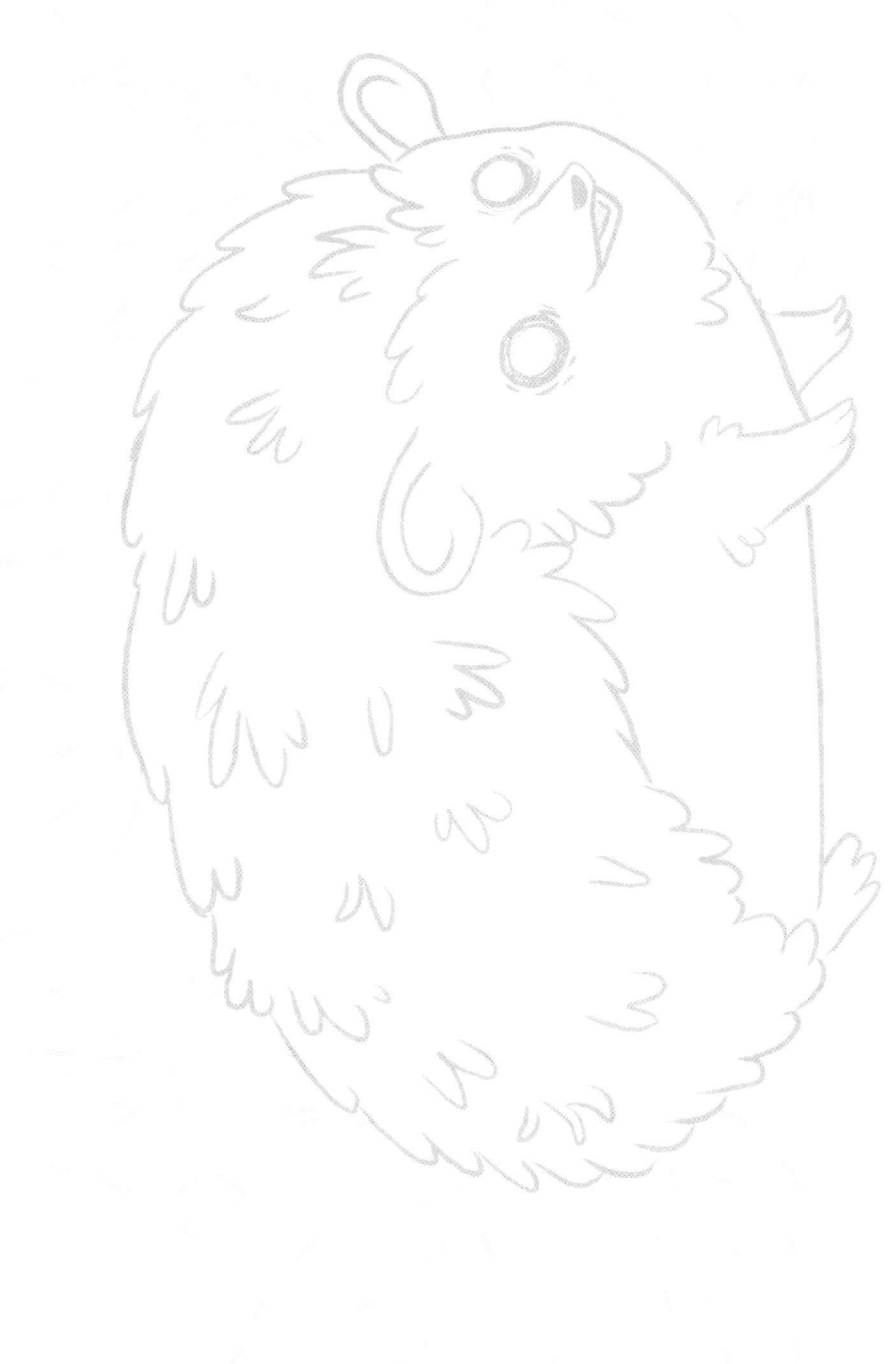

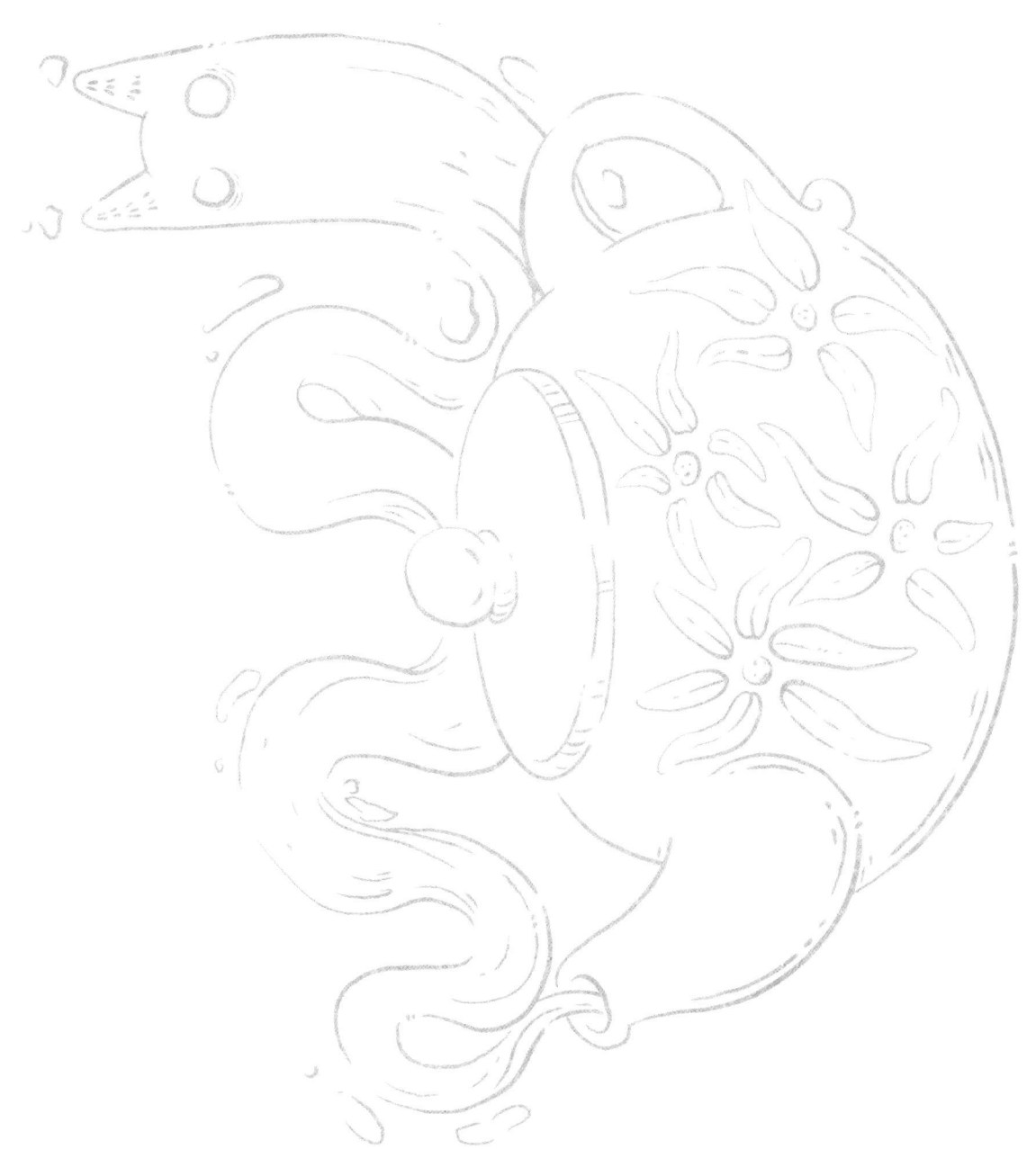

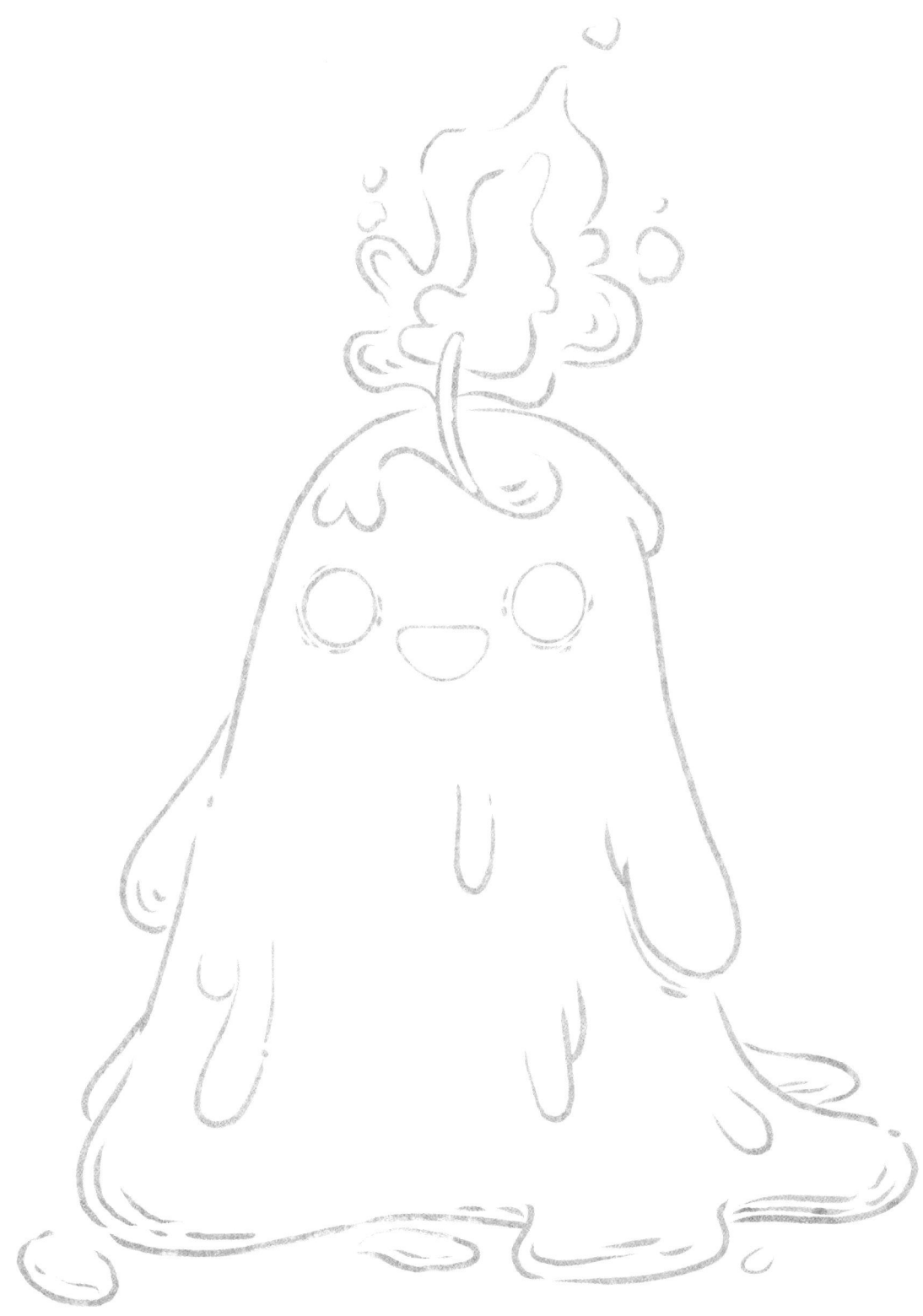

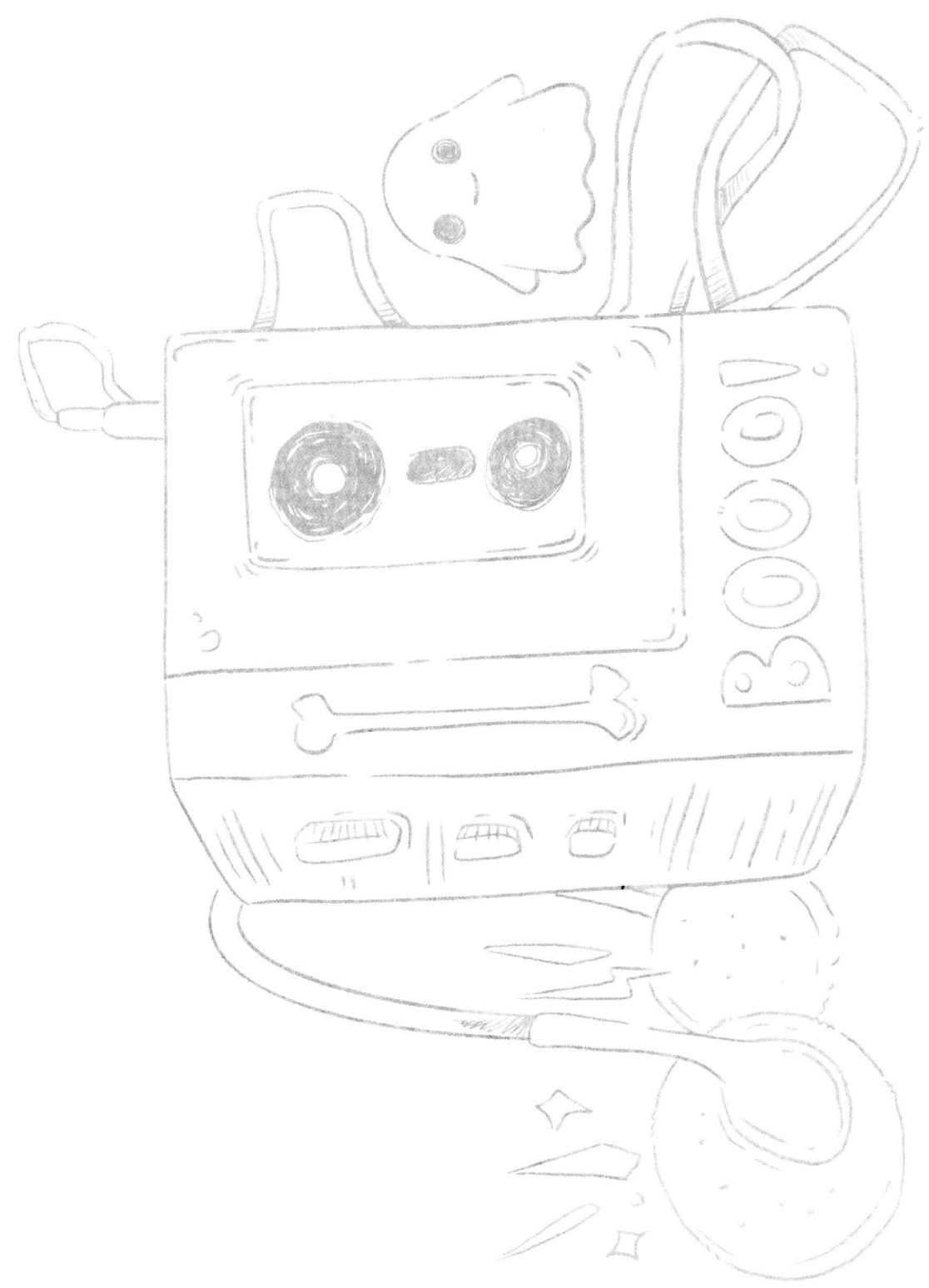

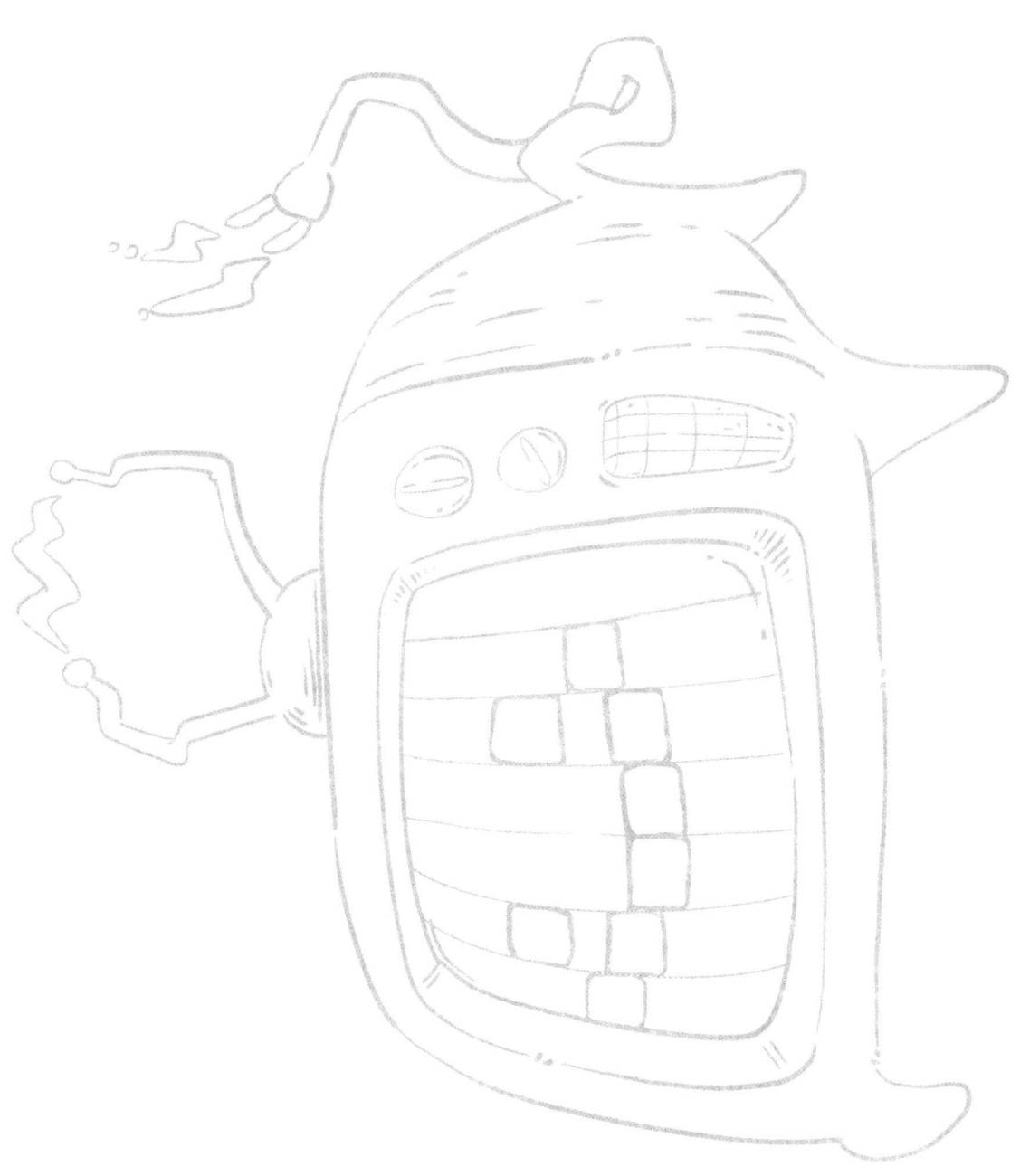

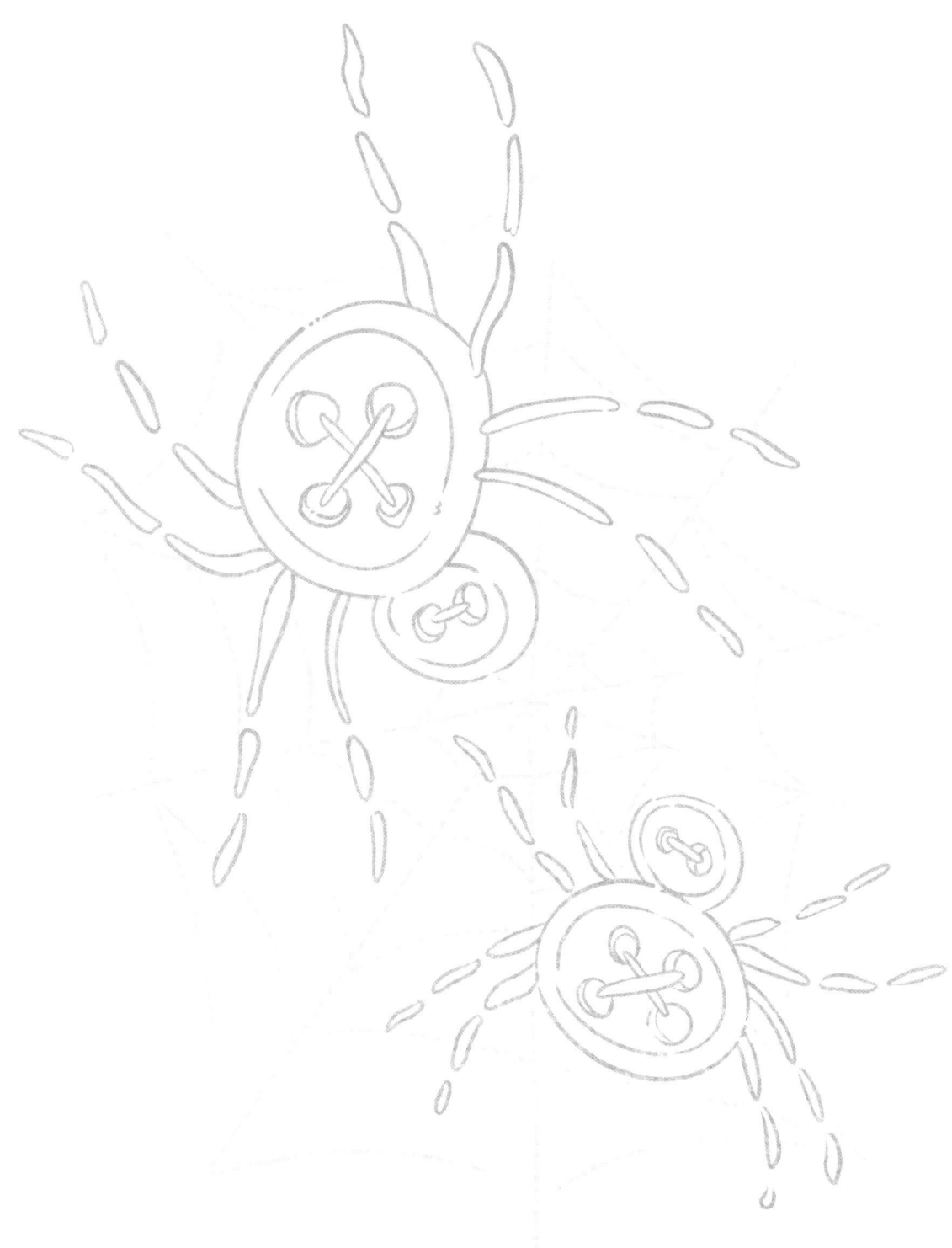

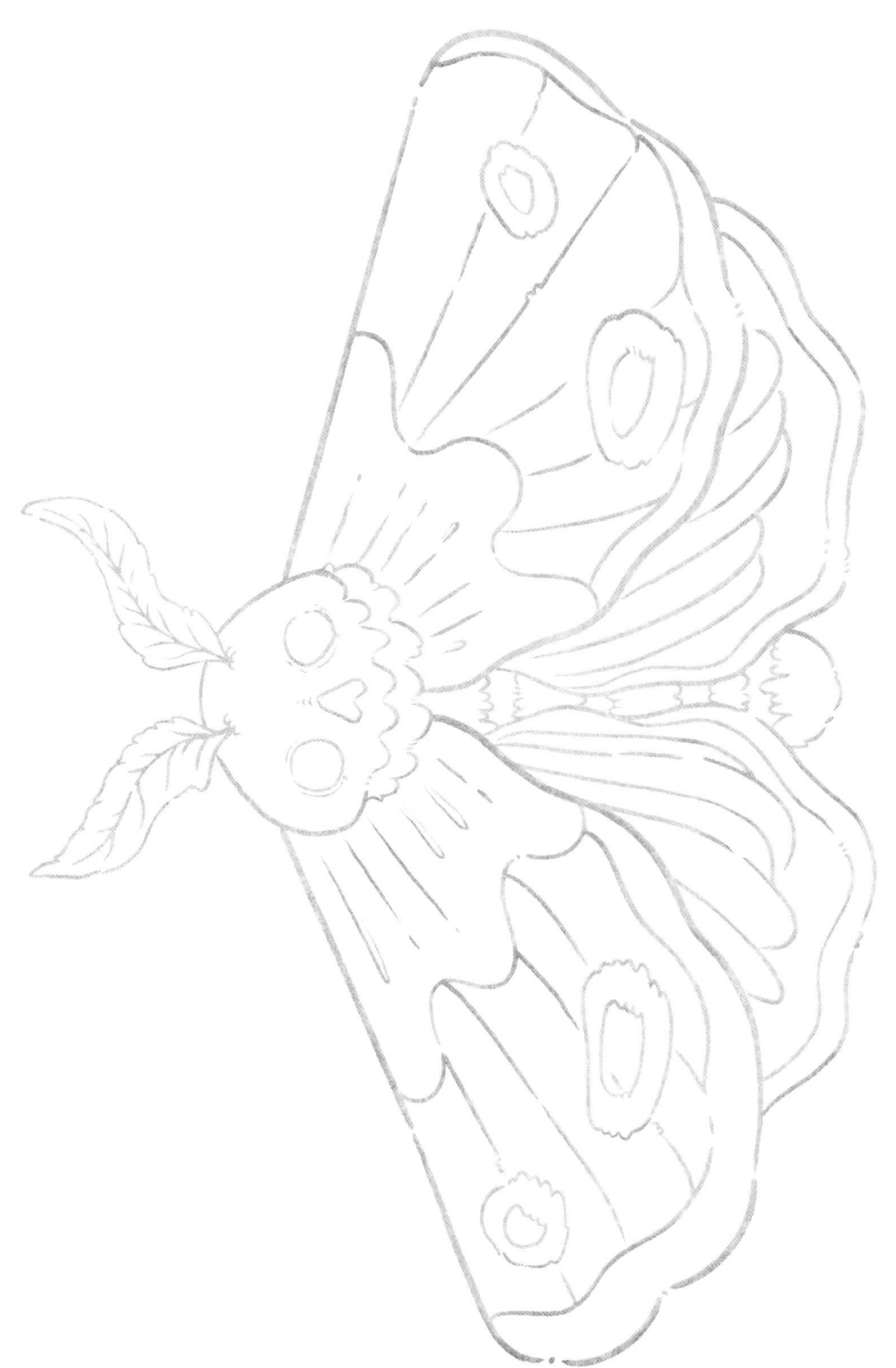

Creepy Cute Watercolor

LEARN TO PAINT
HAUNTINGLY ADORABLE ODDITIES

STEPHANIE BAYLES

Walter Foster

CONTENTS

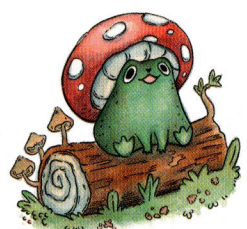

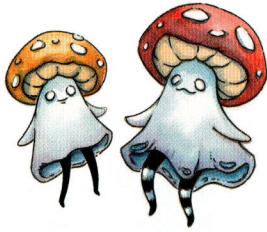

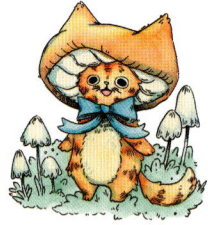

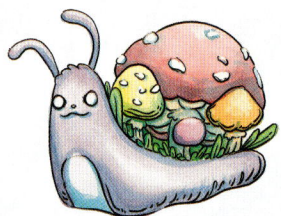

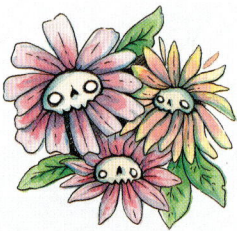

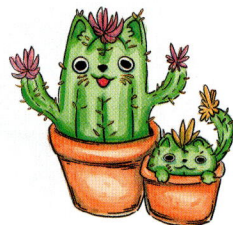

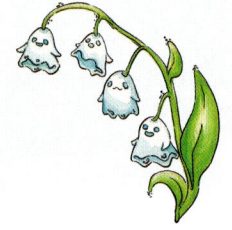

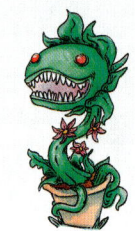

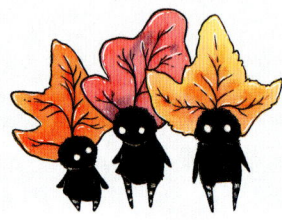

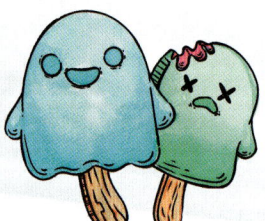

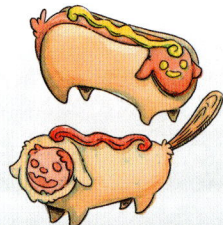

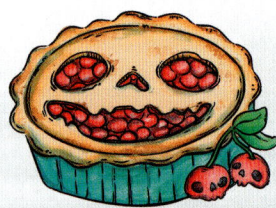

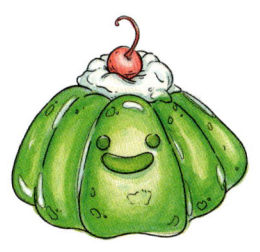
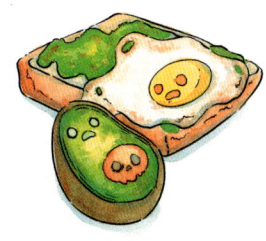
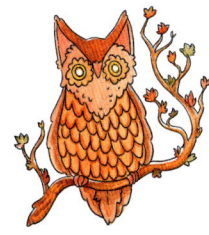
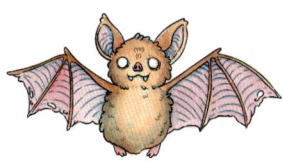
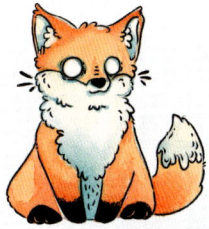
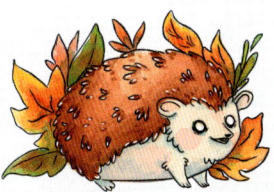
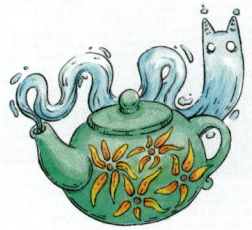
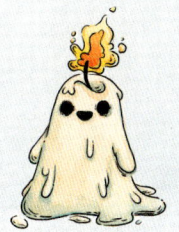
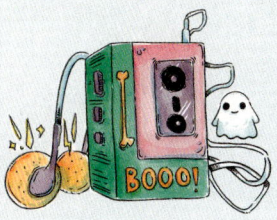
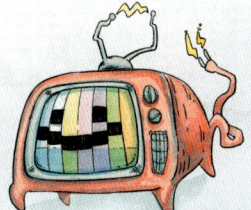
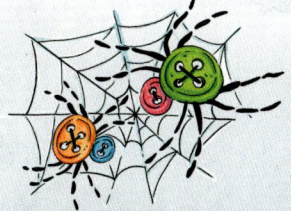
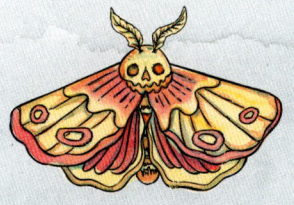

INTRODUCTION

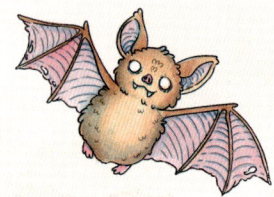

Welcome to my creepy cute watercolor world! It's the place where ghosts proudly sport mushroom caps and TVs have a smiley mind of their own. Around here, ghouls hang out in the garden, food has personality, and every shadow has a story to tell (usually with cat ears).

I created this book for anyone who wants to dip their brush into the bizarre, the whimsical, and the wonderfully weird. Whether you're a total beginner or a seasoned maker of oddities, you'll find step-by-step paintings, helpful tips, and little sparks of strange inspiration throughout these pages.

There's no pressure to be perfect—just permission to get messy, experiment wildly, and paint outside the lines (sometimes literally). Let your inner goblin run free, your paint water get murky, and your spooky side shine.

So, summon your supplies, light your favorite candle (bonus points if it's shaped like a ghost), and let's make some delightfully eerie art together.

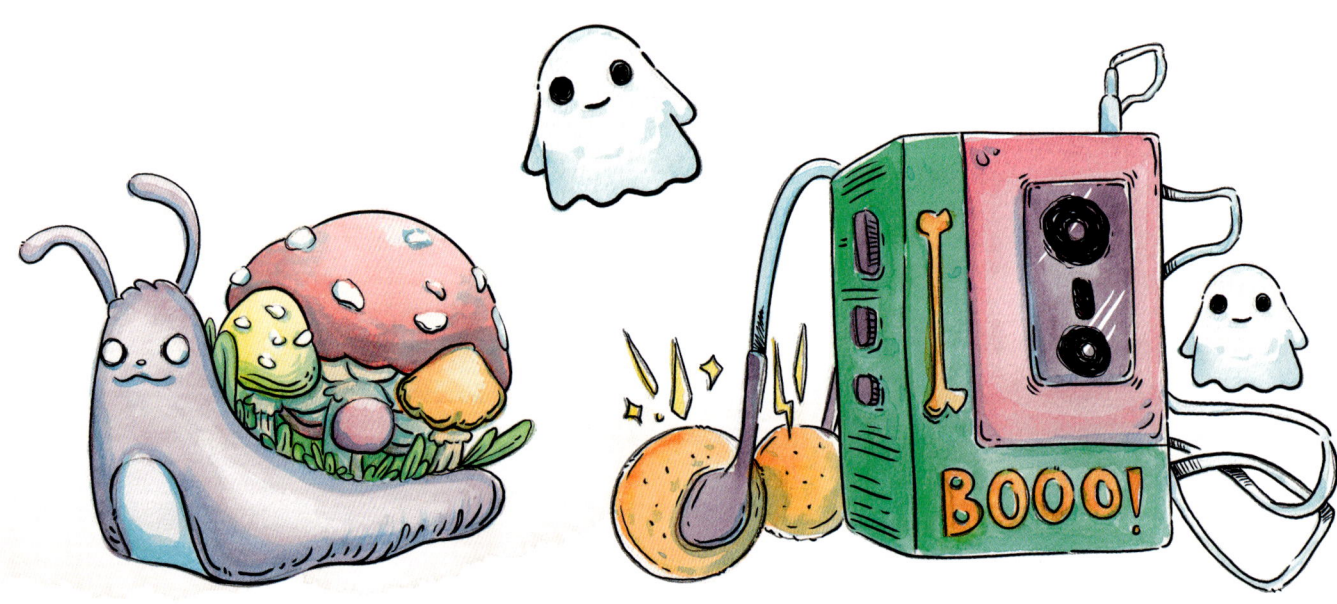

HOW TO USE THIS BOOK

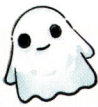

Before you dive headfirst into painting your own haunted mushrooms or possessed pastries, take a little stroll through these first few pages—your trusty tool kit for weird and wonderful watercoloring.

Tools & Supplies: This section lays out all the magical implements you'll need, from brushes and paints to paper and palette. Nothing fancy—just the essentials (plus anything that makes your dark little art heart happy).

Watercolor Basics: New to watercolor? Not sure what a wash is (besides what your laundry's waiting for)? No worries. Here you'll find bite-size tips and easy demos to help you tame your paints and summon texture, blending, and ghastly dead eyes.

Step-by-Step Projects: Each project comes with clear, illustrated instructions so you can follow along one spooky cute step at a time. Think of them as potions: start with a sketch, stir in some color, finish with a flourish of fun.

Watercolor Paper Pad: Flip to the back and you'll find preprinted sketches on real watercolor paper—perfect for jumping in without having to draw a thing. Use them for painting, coloring, or whatever you desire.

Extras: When you've painted your way through the twenty-plus sketches and tutorials in this book, I've got a boatload of extra characters waiting for your imagination and brushes to bring them to life. These don't have step-by-step tutorials; they're to show off all you learned! Simply download the sketch using the QR code provided with the extras and continue on your creepy cute journey.

Most importantly: There are no rules. Want to start in the middle? Do it. Prefer to color with markers instead of paint? Go wild. Paint your ghost cats rainbow? YES. This book is your creative playground, no perfectionism required. Just grab your brush and make something weird and wonderful.

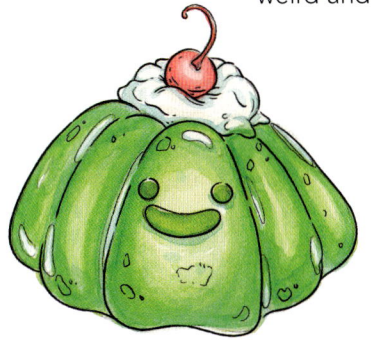

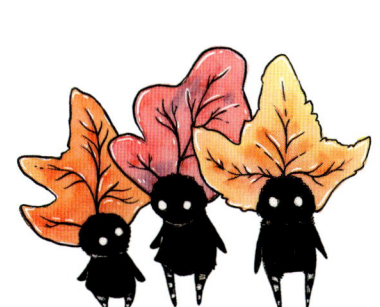

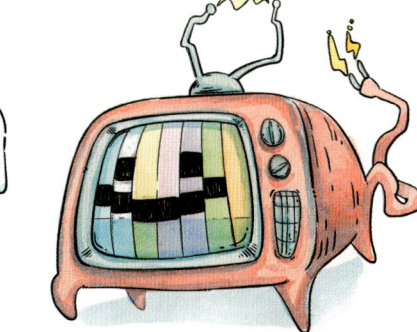

TOOLS & SUPPLIES

Watercolor is a great way to explore your artistic side without a huge investment in special tools or fancy supplies. Here, I've outlined my favorite things to use when painting creepy cute characters. You can find these online, at your local craft store, or at your local art supply shop.

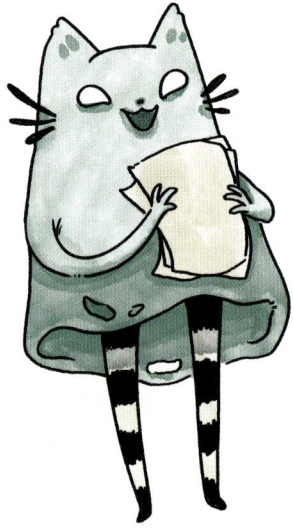

WATERCOLOR PAPER

This book includes a practice pad of watercolor paper to get you started right away. However, if you want to up your watercolor game, you should consider investing in high-quality watercolor paper.

It's very important to pick out a good paper when working with watercolors. If the paper is not meant for a water-based paint, it will tear or warp, so make sure to pay attention when choosing your paper. The paper's label will say if it is meant for watercolor.

TYPES OF PAPER

There are a few different types of watercolor papers. A fun way I like to remember the differences is to think about how the desert is "hot and flat," whereas the mountains are "cold and textured." The same applies to paper!

Hot-press paper is smooth, and really good for adding ink and other media to your artwork. It's also good when working with watercolor pencils.

Cold-press paper is a more textured paper. It holds and absorbs the water and pigment better than hot press. This paper is great for blending colors.

Rough paper is similar to cold-press paper but has more texture.

PAPER WEIGHT

The thickness of your paper plays a big part in your painting. A thin or lightweight paper will warp or buckle easily. The higher the number, the thicker your paper. Try to get a paper that is no smaller then 90 lb.

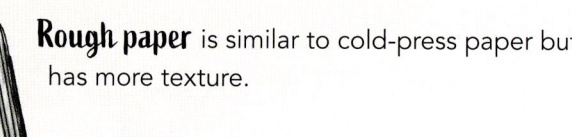

LOOSE SHEETS, PADS & BLOCKS

You can buy individual watercolor paper sheets, or you can get a paper pad meant for watercolor. I think when you are first starting out, a paper pad is the way to go. That way you have more practice pages.

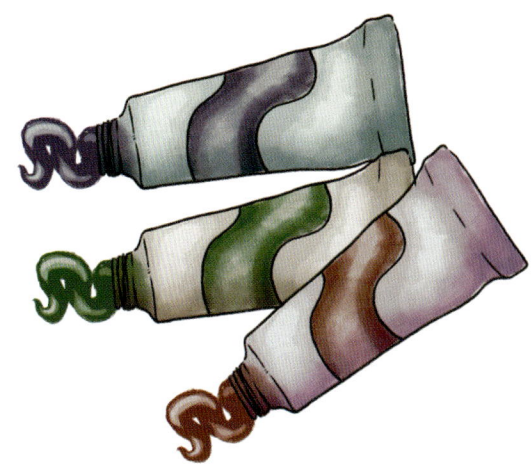

Watercolor blocks are great for painting if you don't want your paper to buckle. The edges of multiple paper pages are glued together. Paint on the top paper, and when you're done, you can cut around the edges and reveal a new, clean watercolor paper page.

WATERCOLOR PAINTS

PALETTE SETS

Some watercolor sets come in a palette. Almost everyone knows this type of watercolor paint. Remember the classic Crayola watercolor sets in elementary school? When you're just getting started, I recommend finding a set with a large variety of colors. This will allow you to experiment with mixing colors and creating the values you want.

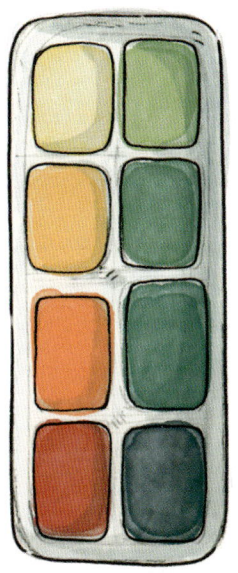

For the paintings in this book, I use Winsor & Newton watercolor paints. See the range of colors on page 14.

TUBES OF PAINT

Tube paint is my preferred form of watercolor paints. Put a small dot of paint on your palette and mix it with water. If the paint dries, more water can be added to reactivate it.

WATERCOLOR PENCILS

Another tool I enjoy working with is watercolor pencils. They are similar to colored pencils, but after coloring in your image, you take a wet brush over the color to turn it into paint—it's practically magic! I especially love this technique because it creates little mess, but for the purpose of this book I suggest sticking with a palette set or collecting tubes of paint.

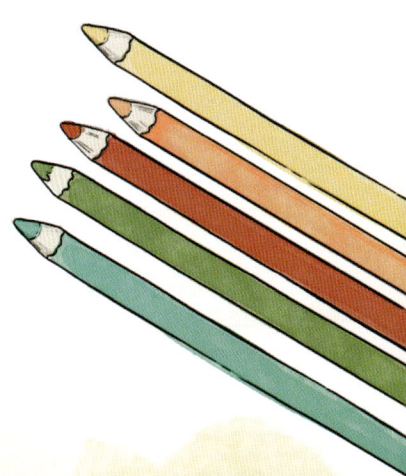

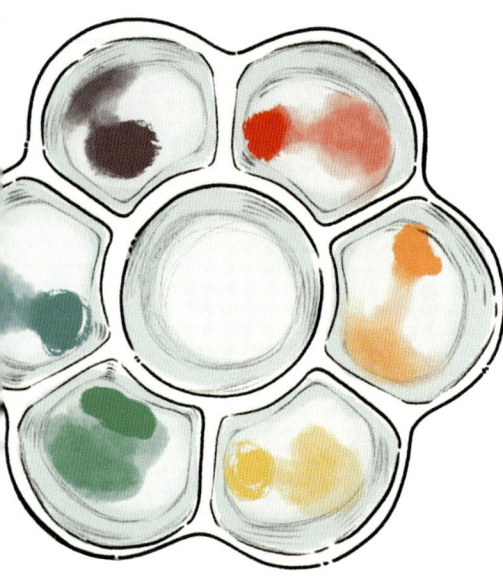

MIXING PALETTE

Always use a mixing palette when mixing your colors with water. I try to use mixing palettes with a slope to them, so I can add the color toward the top of the slope and have the water at the bottom. I find this makes it easier to add the appropriate amount of color to the mix.

BRUSHES

There are many different types of watercolor brushes to choose from, with a wide range of price points. I recommend getting the best brushes you can afford. If your budget is tight, the main thing to focus on is the brush tip. You want the tip to come to a point and not fray out.

For the creepy cute paintings in this book, I suggest you have the following brushes on hand:

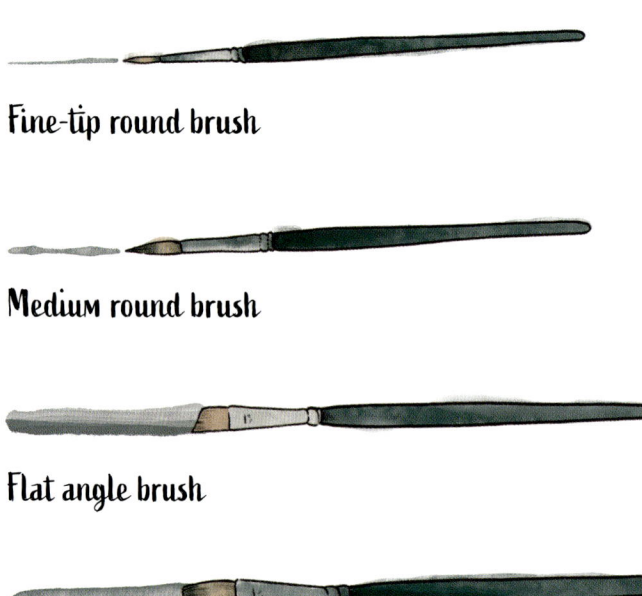

Fine-tip round brush

Medium round brush

Flat angle brush

Flat brush

WATER

Obviously, you'll need water to paint with watercolor. Make sure to always have at least two cups of water at your workstation: one to clean your brush in between colors, and one to mix and activate your paint.

WATER DROPPER

If you don't want to use a brush to carry the water from your jar to your palette, you can use a water dropper.

PAPER TOWELS

Always have some paper towels at your painting station. Use them to clean your brushes or dry them if you applied too much water. You can also use paper towel to blot your painting and add some fun effects.

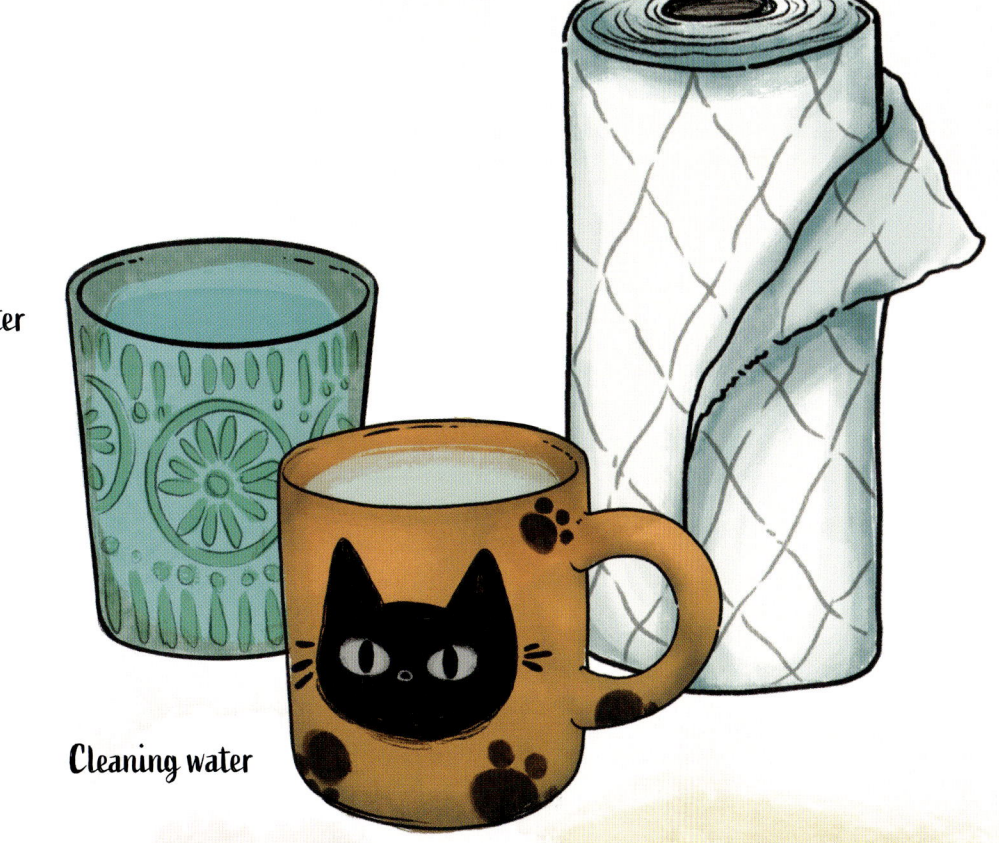

Mixing water

Cleaning water

PENS & PENCILS

PENCILS

When first starting, you'll lightly sketch your image with a pencil—a 2H pencil works best. Don't press hard on your paper when sketching. You want the sketch lines to be very light. I would avoid a mechanical pencil for your sketching.

PENS

I love using ink and pen in my artwork. I sometimes sketch in ink before watercoloring. Be careful though: some inks smear when mixed with water. You'll see, most of the time I suggest finishing a painting by outlining it in pen once the piece is dry. It really helps the finished work pop!

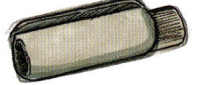

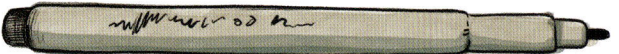

Micron pens: These work well for initial sketches and fine-line details when you're done.

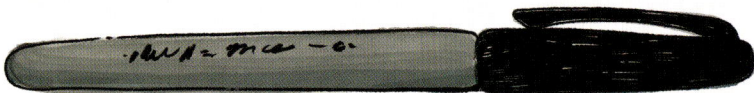

Permanent markers: For bolder outlines, a permanent marker works best.

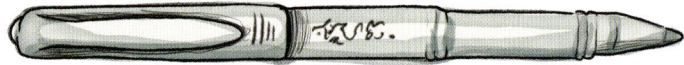

White pens: White pens are great for adding highlights to your image after you are done painting. My favorite is the Uni-Ball white pen.

WATERCOLOR BASICS

Once you have all your supplies ready, it's time to watercolor! In this section, I'm sharing the basic techniques I use to paint creepy cute characters. You can follow along and paint as I do, or skip to the fun part and just start painting.

BRUSH POSITION

When learning to watercolor, brush position can be tricky. After a few practice strokes, you'll discover that you want to use the side of the brush, not the tip. Meaning, you're not holding the brush straight up and down, perpendicular to the paper. Instead, you hold it at an angle—with a comfortable grip—using the body of the bristles.

WASHES

"Wash" is a term you'll see often in watercolor tutorials. There are several styles of washes, including *flat* (a solid color), *gradient* (a solid color that changes from light to dark), and *variegated* or *blended* (a wash with more than one color). A wash is a fast and effective way to fill a background with color and can also be used to fill in large areas of a sketch.

Watercolor is all about transparency, so always start light and build up gradually. Begin with a diluted wash (lots of water, just a little pigment) and let it dry completely before adding deeper colors on top.

To lighten a color, simply add more water. To darken it, use less water and more color—there's no need to reach for black. Most watercolor sets include a tube of white, but try to avoid it. In traditional watercolor, your highlights come from the white of the paper itself, left intentionally unpainted.

Let each layer dry before adding the next, and remember: every new layer should deepen the color and add dimension, not cover up what's underneath.

ACTIVATE YOUR PAINT

Whether using tubes of watercolor or a palette with dry watercolor blocks, you need to activate the paint. You can use water droppers, a wet brush, or a spray bottle with clean water.

Gradient wash

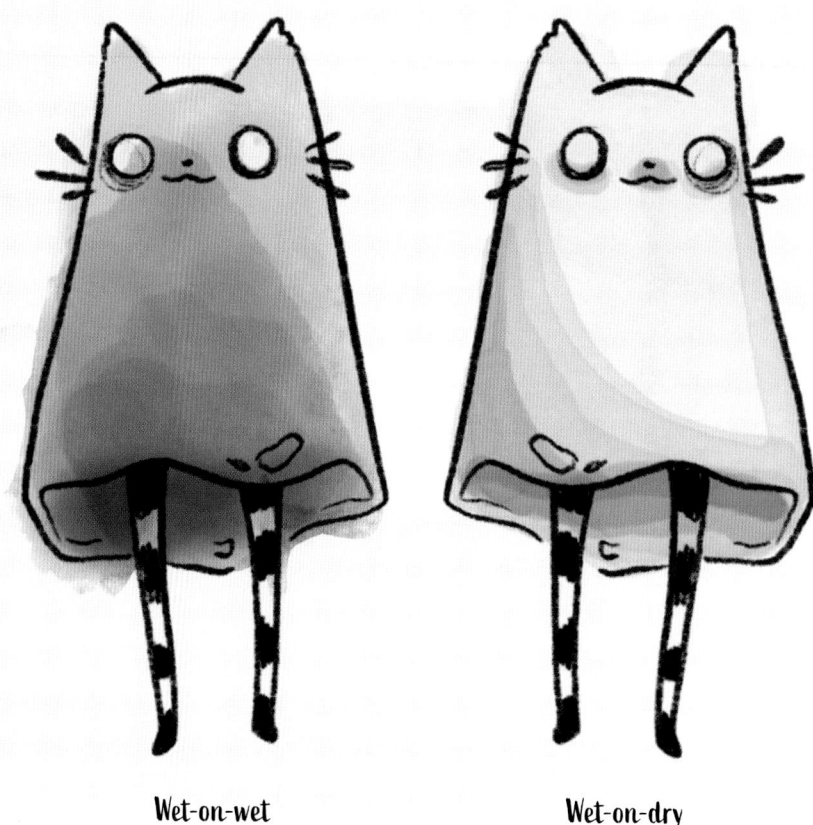

Wet-on-wet   Wet-on-dry

WET-ON-WET

For the wet-on-wet technique you apply a wet brush on a wet surface. First you want to use a clean brush to apply water to your paper. While the paper is still wet, take your wet brush with color and paint it on the paper. The water helps the paint disperse onto the paper. This technique is great for doing light backgrounds, as well as easily blending colors and creating gradient effects.

WET-ON-DRY

For the wet-on-dry technique you apply your wet brush loaded with color to dry paper. The wet-on-dry technique is used to create darker, saturated colors and crisp lines between layers of paint.

LAYERING

As we've discussed, watercolor is about transparency, which means colors can be layered to achieve interesting effects. As you work through the projects in this book, you'll use layering a lot. Initially, you'll layer a single color to create depth. Then, you'll layer in other, sometimes unexpected, colors to create interesting shadows.

Look closely at the highlights and shadows on our foxy friend. The lightest orange areas are a single layer of burnt sienna and cadmium yellow; the deeper shades of orange have additional layers. The shadows throughout his white fur are done in blue.

LIFTING

As you practice washes, we-on-wet, and wet-on-dry, at some point you're bound to have too much water. You can use paper towel to carefully "lift" water out of the painting and soak up the excess water. You must act fast though! This is another reason to keep paper towels on hand.

You can also use a paper towel or clean brush to lift color when it's too dark. Simply add more water to lighten the dark color before drying it up with the towel. Too much water should be avoided, though. Overly saturated paper, even watercolor paper, can rip and tear.

Lifting is a way to add texture to your work as well. You can intentionally "blot" your painting to lift out color and leave the texture of the paper behind.

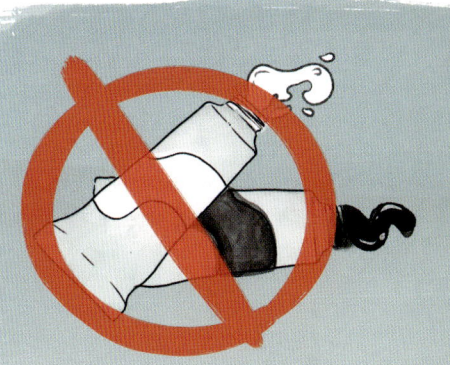

NO BLACK OR WHITE

When watercolor painting, white and black pigments don't work the same way as they do in traditional paints. Avoid them. Instead, add more layers of pigment to darken colors and use a white pen to add highlights.

DRY BRUSH

Another way to add texture to paint is with a dry brush. As it sounds, this technique uses very little water and a lot of paint. It can be an interesting way to add depth to the bark of a rotting log or fur on a hedgehog.

A dry brush can be used to create splatter too! To add a random sprinkling of color, use a dry brush loaded with just a touch of color and "flick" the bristles toward the painting.

CLEAN UP

The last step of any watercolor session is cleaning up. When you are finished with your painting, clean off your brush under the faucet until no more color comes out of the brush. Always store your brushes bristles up to avoid damaging them.

COLOR PALETTE DETAILS

For the projects in this book, I use Winsor & Newton's Cotman watercolor paints. The swatches shown here feature the colors I use repeatedly when painting creepy cute. You should use whatever brand of paints you like, and if you don't have the same color, try to match it as best you can.

I suggest testing your colors on scrap paper or creating a color swatch sheet for reference. I use a watercolor sketchbook to test and write down the colors I am using. I also use this sketchbook for mixing colors and taking notes.

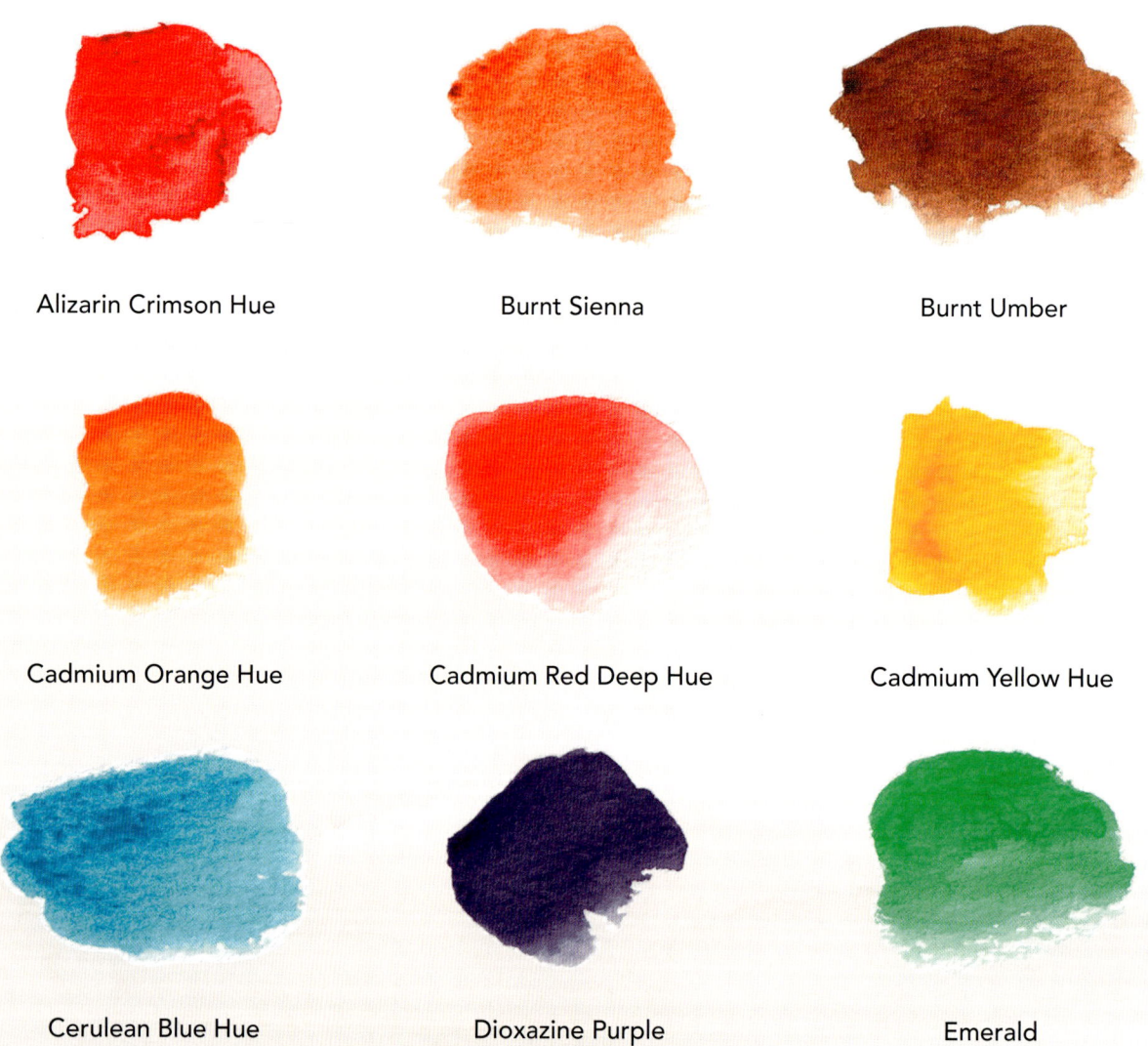

Alizarin Crimson Hue	Burnt Sienna	Burnt Umber
Cadmium Orange Hue	Cadmium Red Deep Hue	Cadmium Yellow Hue
Cerulean Blue Hue	Dioxazine Purple	Emerald

Remember, avoid black or white paint. When you are creating shadows, try mixing the color with a dark blue. For highlights, use a white pen or the white of the paper. Build up color values by painting a color on paper, letting it dry, and painting over it again.

MUDDY COLORS

Remember to always clean off brushes when switching colors to avoid accidently mixing and muddying shades.

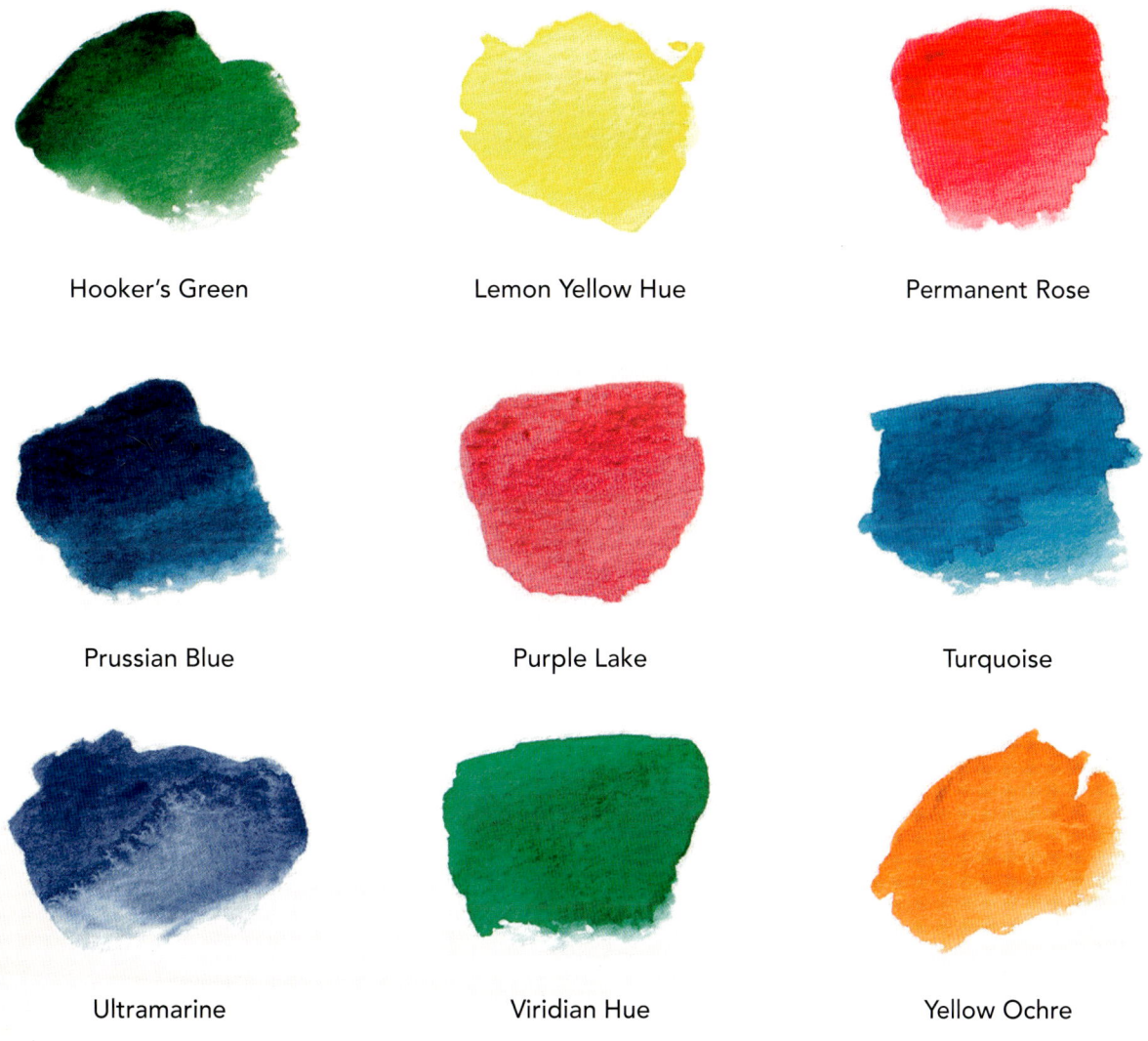

Hooker's Green

Lemon Yellow Hue

Permanent Rose

Prussian Blue

Purple Lake

Turquoise

Ultramarine

Viridian Hue

Yellow Ochre

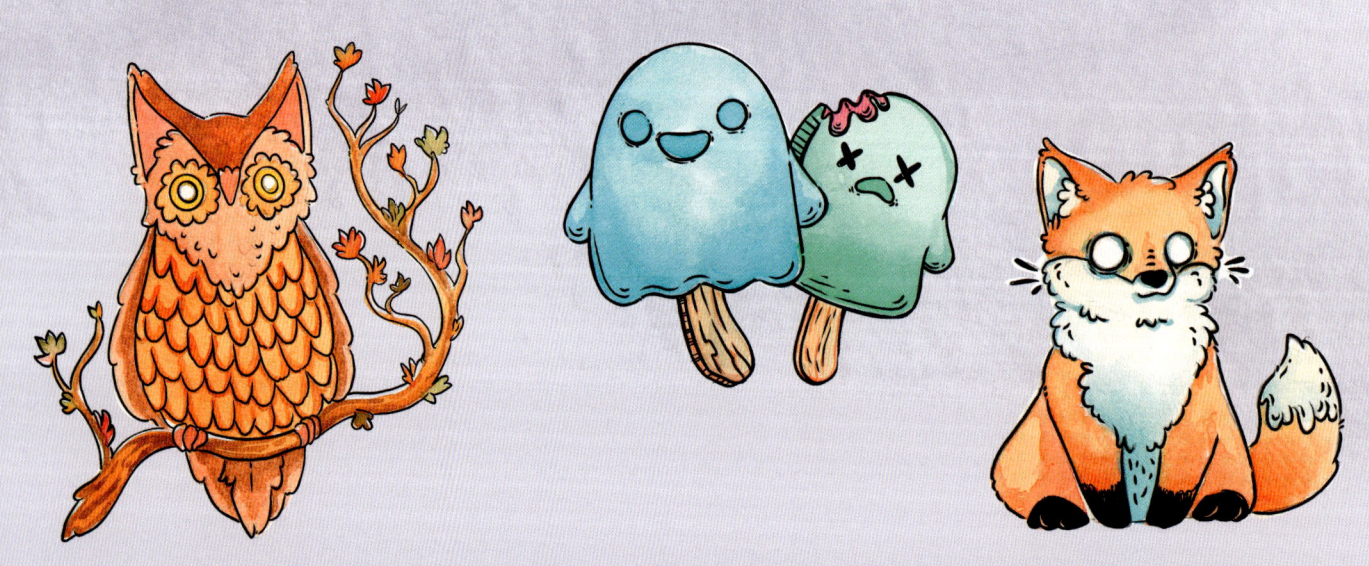

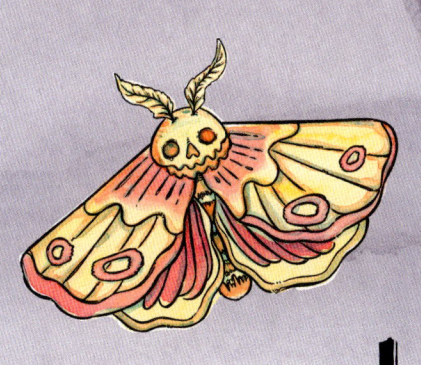

LET'S PAINT CREEPY CUTE CHARACTERS!

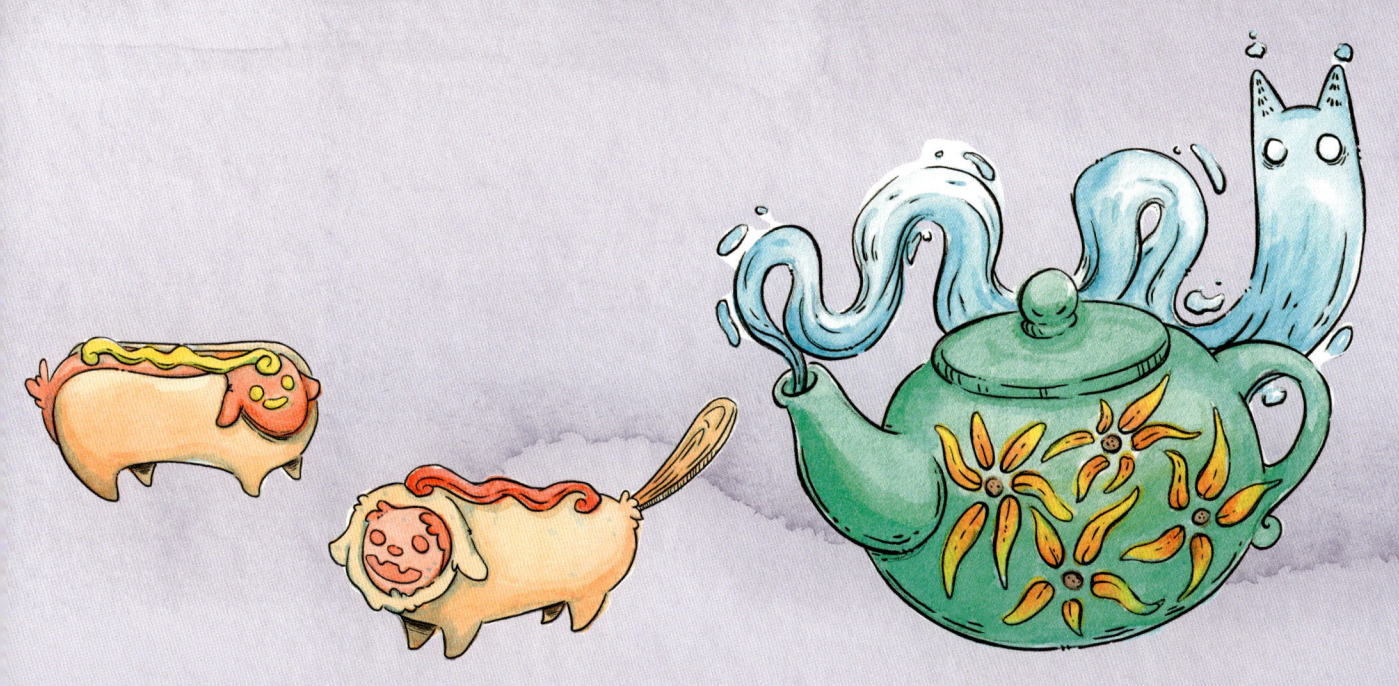

FROG ON A LOG

SUPPLIES

Flat brush
Round brush
Pen to outline

COLORS

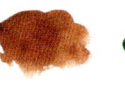

Yellow ochre   Burnt umber   Hooker's green   Alizarin crimson hue   Prussian blue

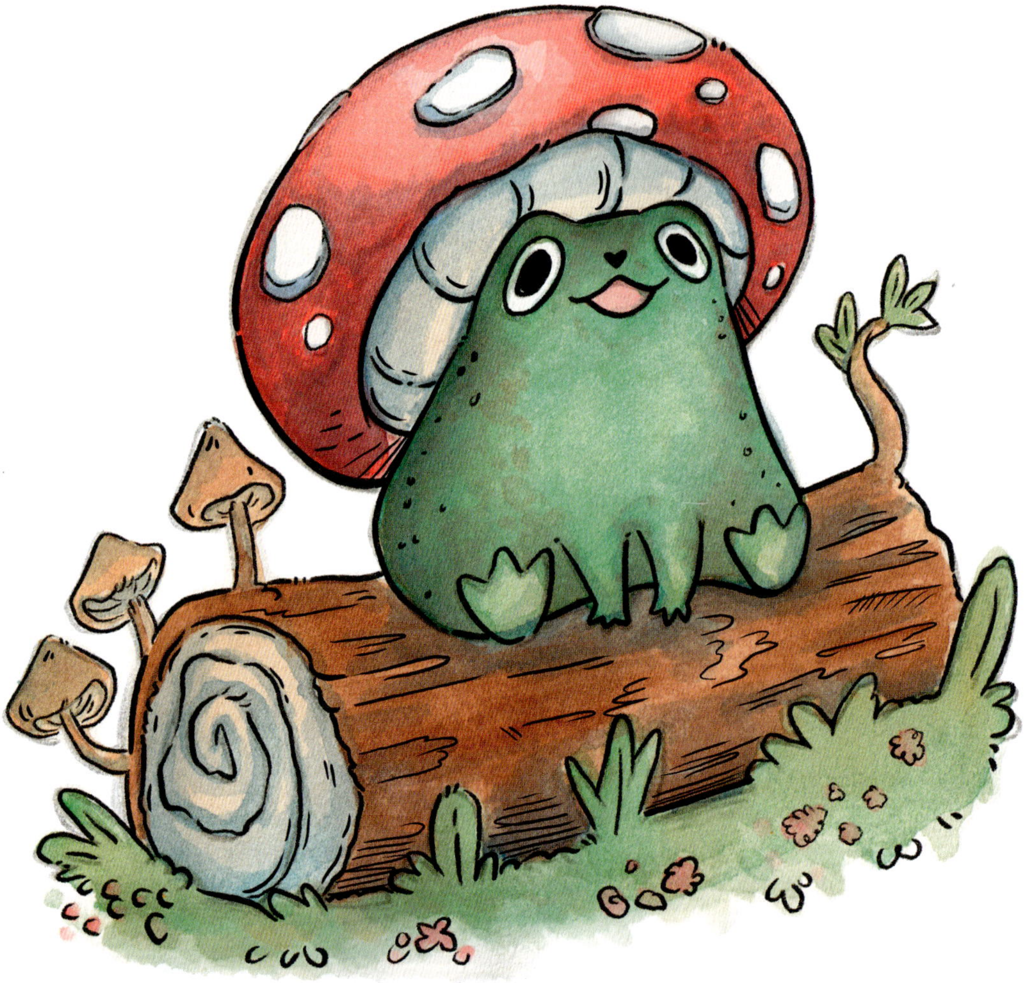

1

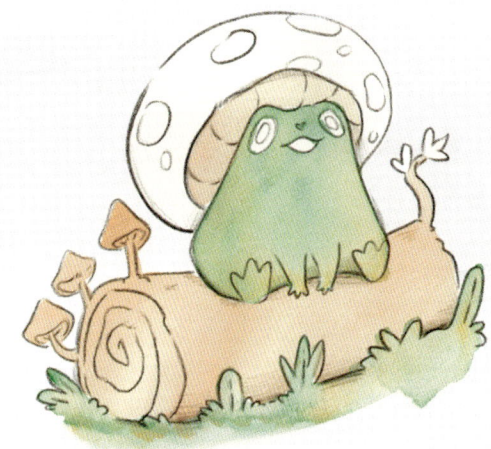

2

3

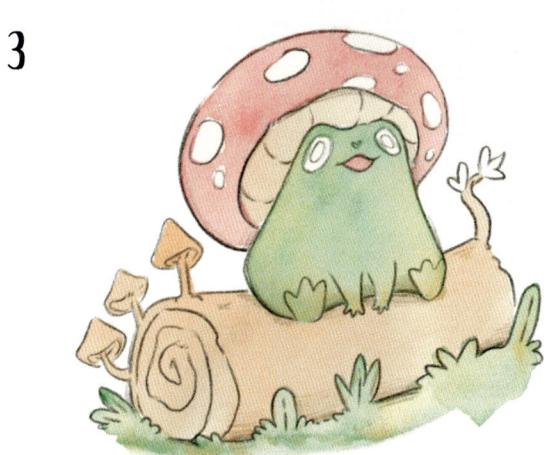

4

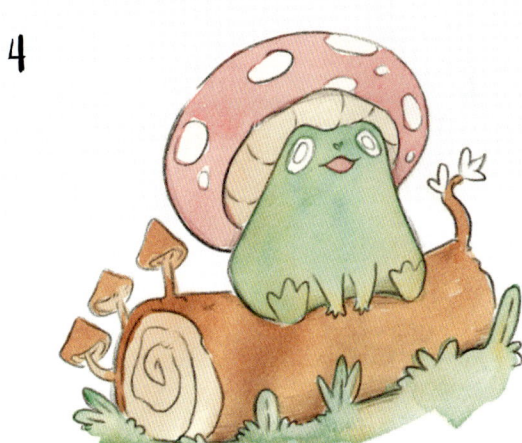

1. Mix yellow ochre and burnt umber and apply a light wash on the dry paper. Fill in the log and the underside of the mushroom cap.

2. Using the wet-on-wet technique, wet the frog's body and the grassy area. Apply a mix of Hooker's green and yellow ochre. Allow to dry.

3. On dry paper, apply a light wash of alizarin crimson hue to the mushroom cap. Make sure to go around the spots, leaving the white of the paper.

4. Dilute burnt umber with water to make it less saturated and apply that to the log and tiny mushroom caps. Avoid filling in the side of the log. Allow to dry.

5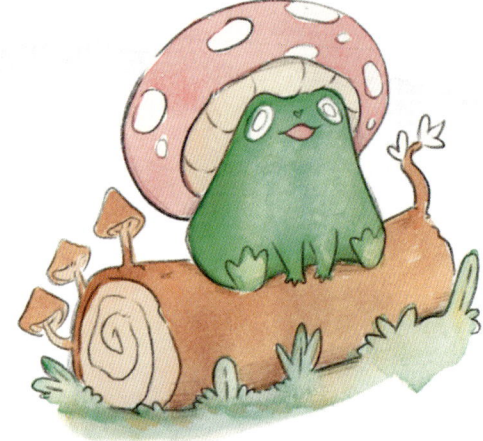

6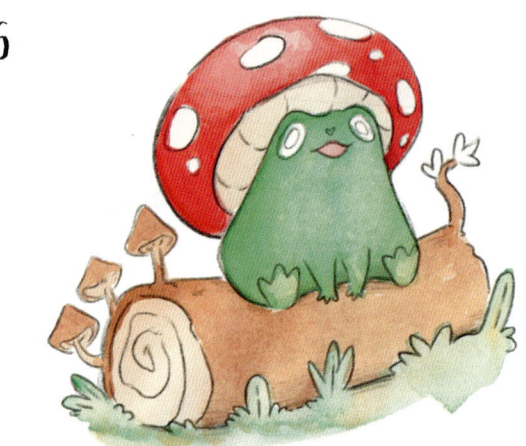

7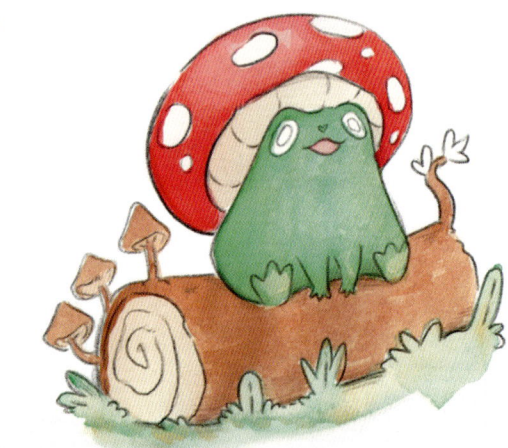

8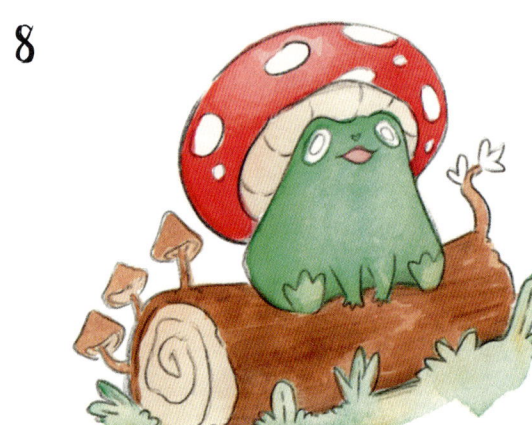

5. Apply Hooker's green to the body of the frog using the wet-on-dry technique. Add the color close to the linework and paint inward to give a gradient effect. The frog's tummy should be lighter than the outline of his body.

6. Deepen the color value on the mushroom cap by layering alizarin crimson hue over the previous wash. In between adding layers, allow the paint to dry a little before adding the next layer, and apply the next layer to the damp paper.

7. Using the flat brush, apply burnt umber to the log using the wet-on-dry technique. Paint streaks/lines. These can be random because we want to add texture to the log and make it look organic. Allow to dry.

8. Continue to add brushstrokes to the log, letting each layer dry before applying a new layer.

9. Using a round brush, dilute burnt umber and add speckles to the side body of the frog.

9

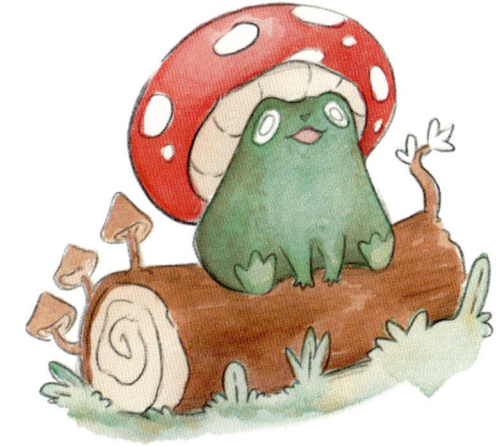

10

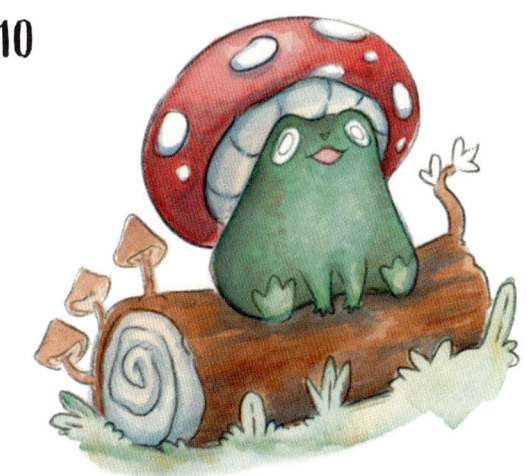

11

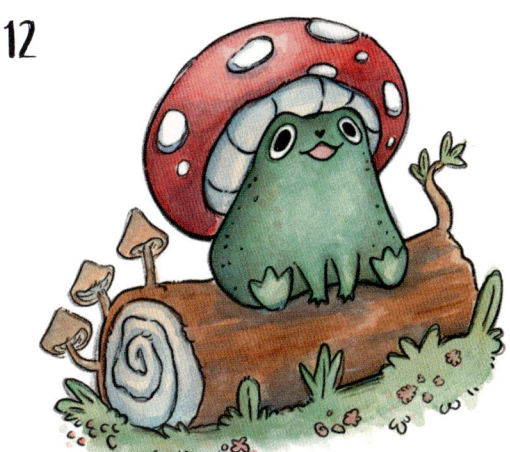

12

10. Time to add some shadows using Prussian blue:

   – Paint a light wash on the mushroom cap.

   – Under the mushroom cap, follow the linework to apply shadow.

   – Follow the swirl of the log to create shadow.

   – Using the flat brush, paint lines on the log while also painting the area of the log that's under the frog.

   – Paint a light wash around the frog's body.

11. Add finishing details. Paint another, darker layer of yellow ochre and Hooker's green on the grass, as well as the tiny leaves on the log. Add some alizarin crimson hue speckles with a dry brush if you want to make it appear there are flowers in the grass.

12. Once completely dry, outline the painting with ink.

MUSH BOOS

SUPPLIES

Flat brush
Fine round brush
Pen to outline

COLORS

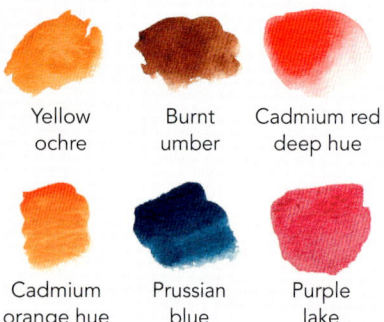

Yellow ochre   Burnt umber   Cadmium red deep hue

Cadmium orange hue   Prussian blue   Purple lake

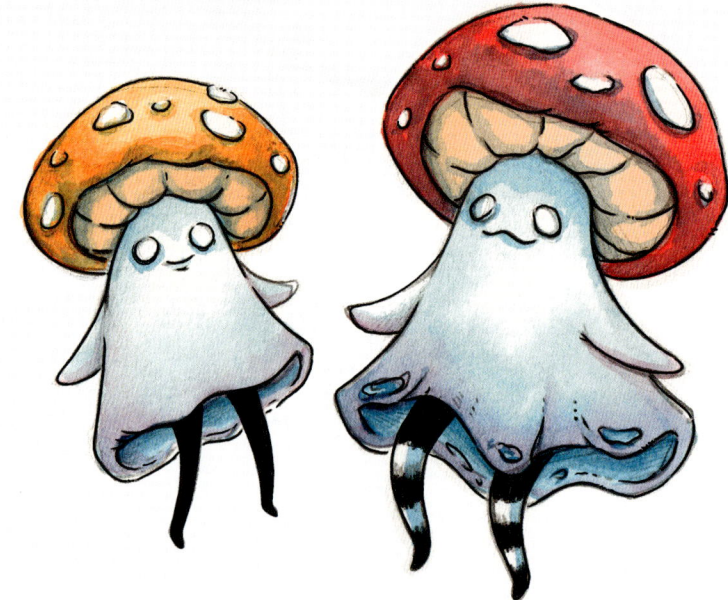

1. Mix yellow ochre and burnt umber together and apply a light wash on the dry paper under the mushroom caps.

   Using cadmium red deep hue, apply a light wash on the dry paper to fill in the top of the right mushroom. Be careful to avoid filling in the white spots.

2. Use the same technique to apply cadmium orange hue to the top of the left mushroom.

3. Using the wet-on-wet technique, fill in the bodies of the ghosts with water and Prussian blue. Work from the bottom of the body toward the head, keeping the most saturated color at the bottom.

   Deepen the color value on the right mushroom cap by painting additional layers of cadmium red deep hue over the previous wash. Between layers, allow the wash to dry until it is just damp before applying the next layer. As you build the layers, leave an area without the extra layers as a spot toward the top reflecting light.

4. Using the wet-on-dry technique, use purple lake to paint shadows along the bottoms of the ghosts. Paint from the bottom to the middle of the body for a gradient effect. Do this on the arms as well.

   Using the wet-on-wet technique with Prussian blue, paint the inside of the ghosts.

5. Time to add some shadows using Prussian blue and a fine round brush:

   - Paint a light wash on the mushroom caps.
   - On the underside of the mushroom caps, apply shadows along the linework.
   - Apply shadows under the eyes and mouth, as well as where the head meets the mushroom.

6. Ink the outline.

1

2

3

4

5

6

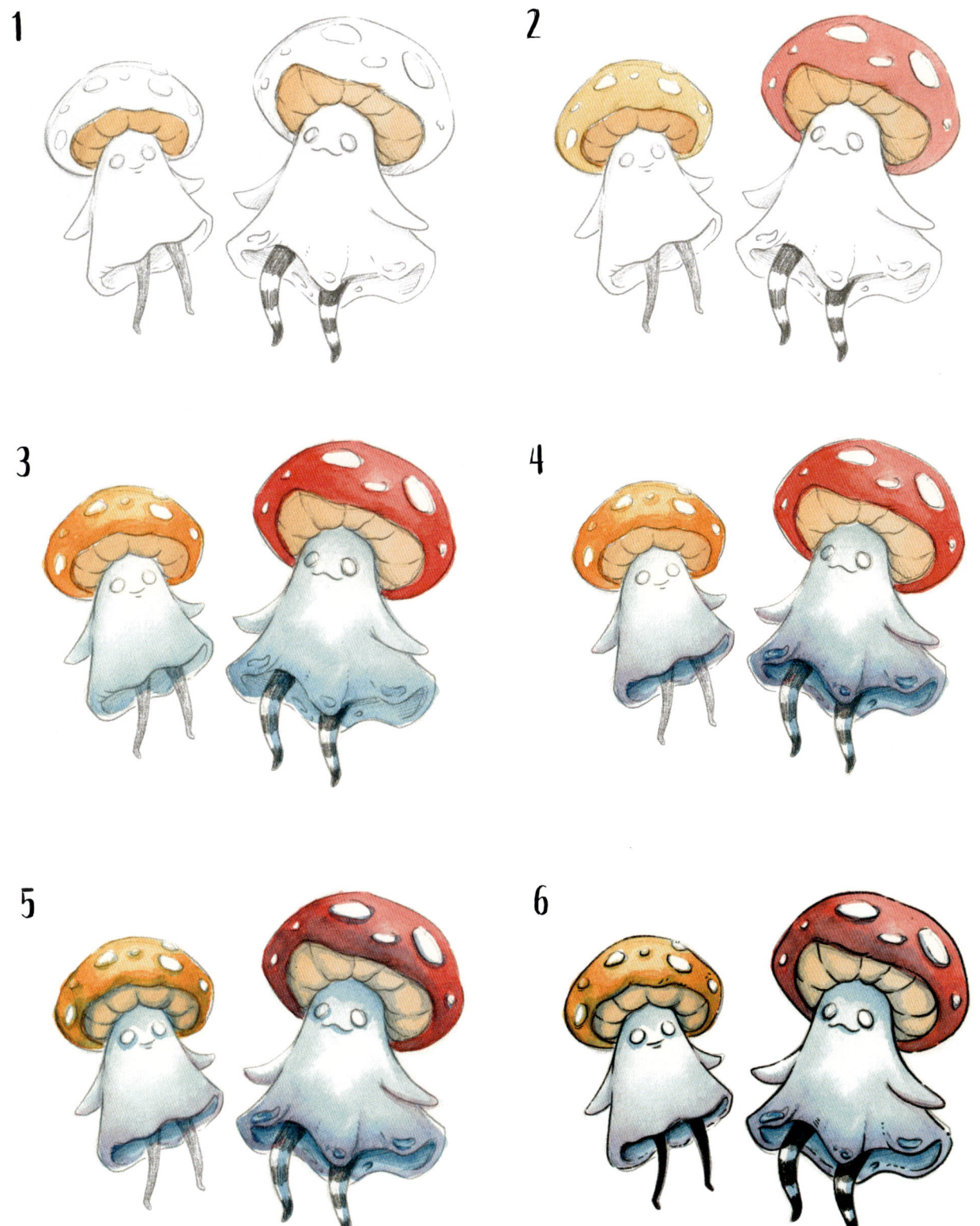

MEOW SHROOM

SUPPLIES

Fine round brush
Medium round brush
Pen to outline

COLORS

 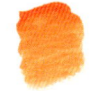   

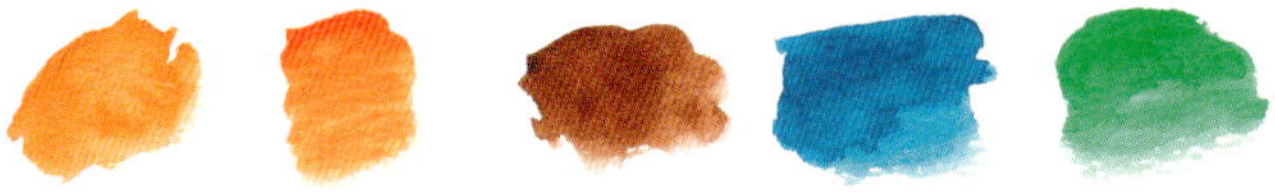

Yellow ochre   Cadmium orange hue   Burnt umber   Turquoise   Emerald

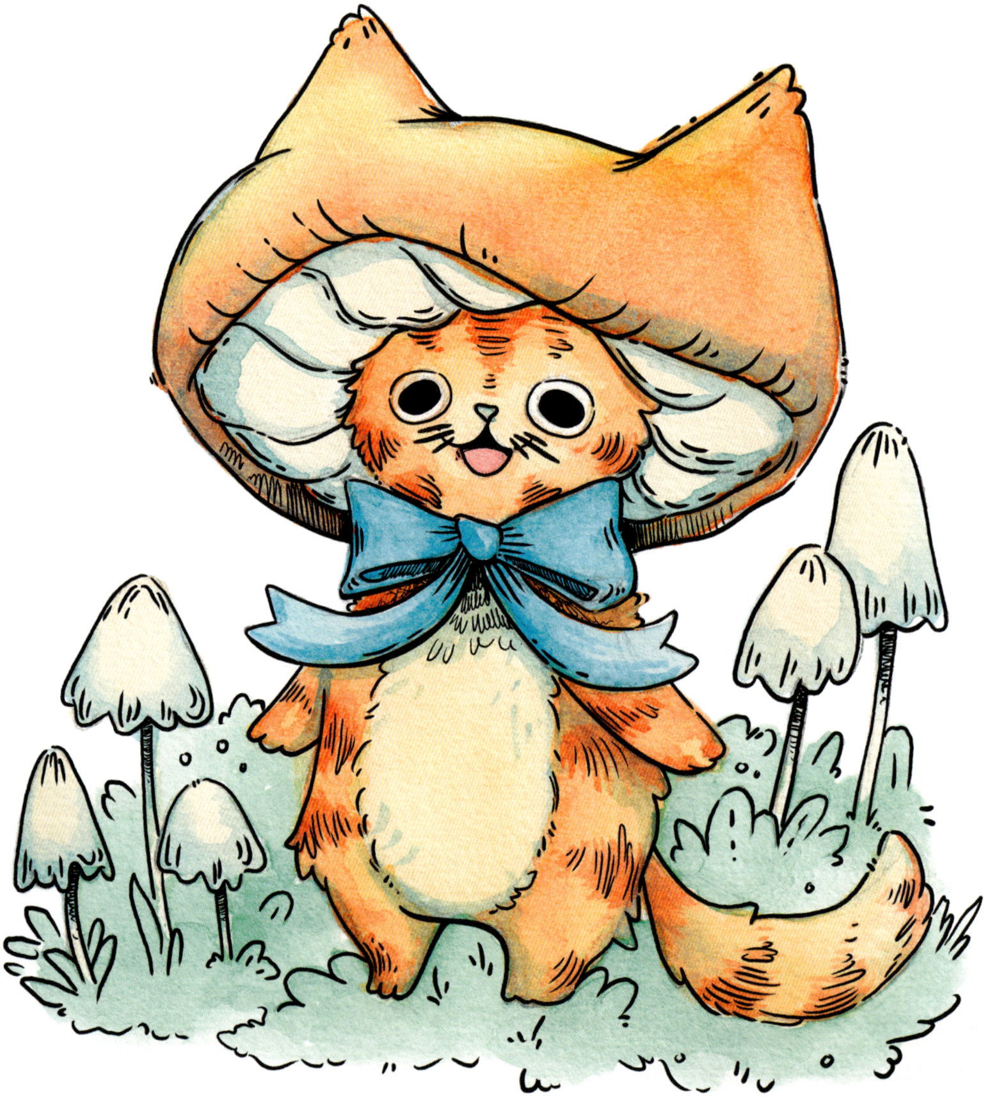

1

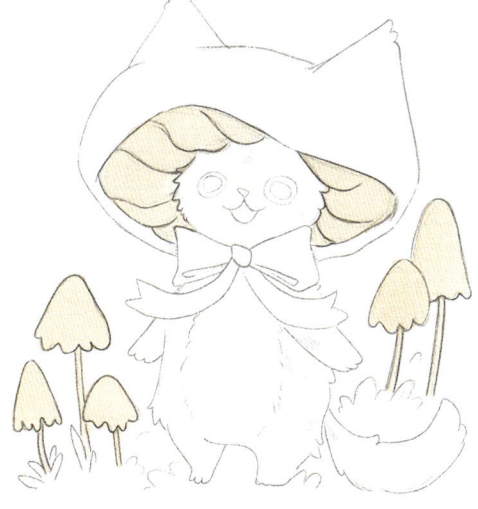

2

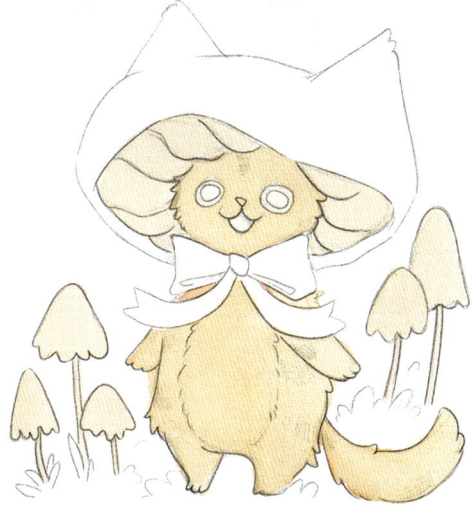

3

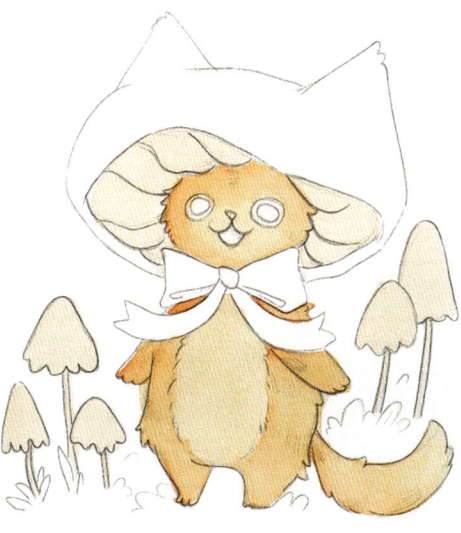

4

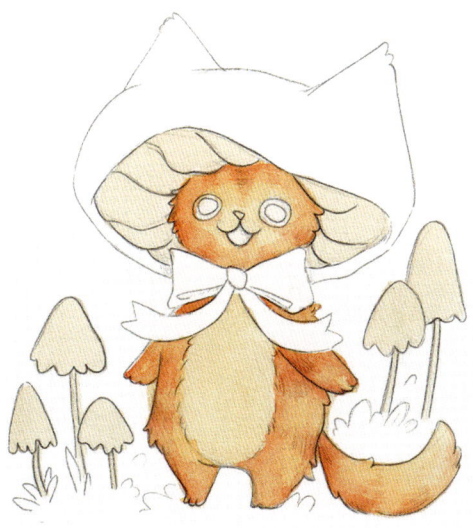

1. Apply a light wash of yellow ochre on the small mushrooms and under the underside of the large mushroom cap. Allow to dry.

2. Apply a wash of cadmium orange hue to the head, body, and tail of the cat, and let dry.

3. Add another layer of cadmium orange hue to the body, but avoid painting the cat's stomach.

4. Using burnt umber and the fine round brush, paint the first layer of stripes on the fur of the cat's forehead, body, and base of the tail.

5

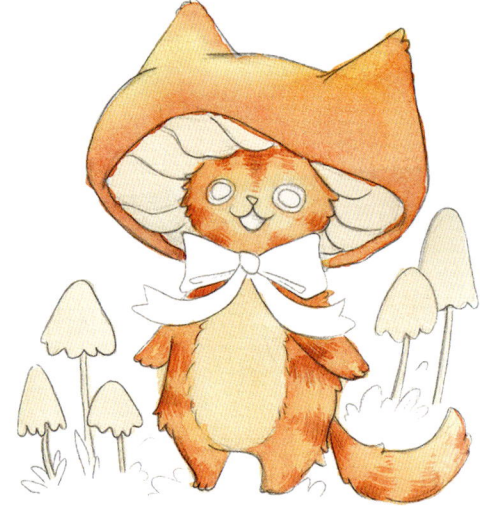

6

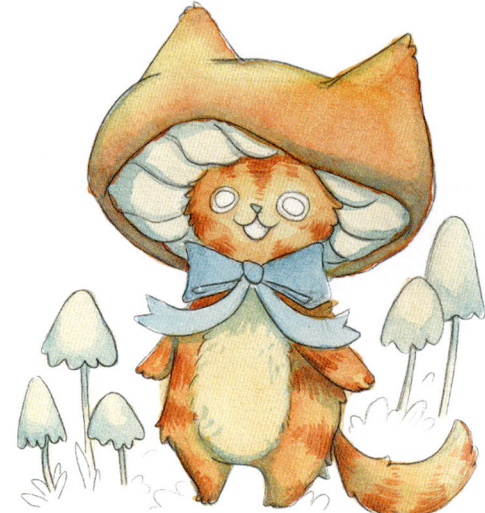

7

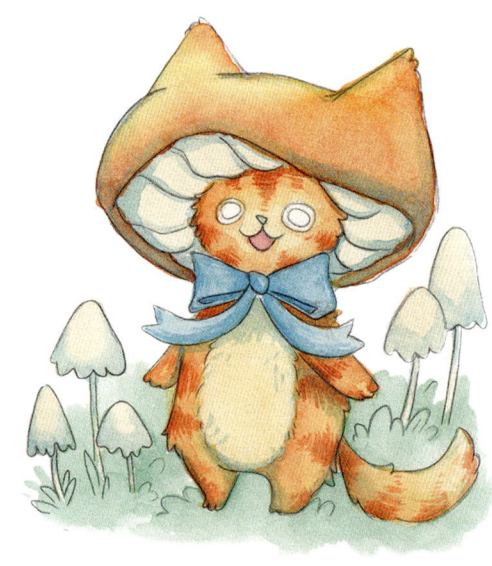

8

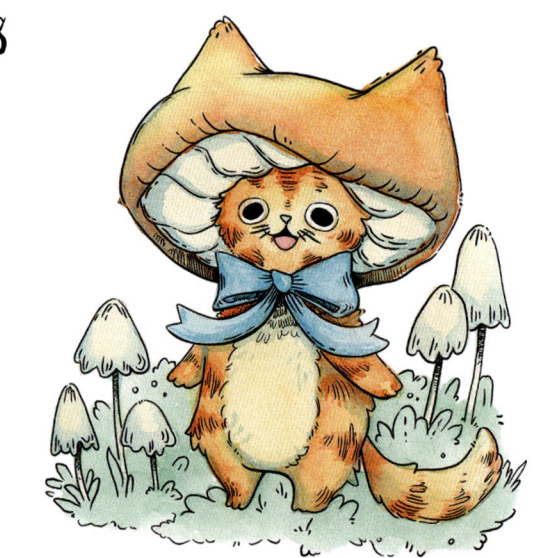

5. Paint the cap of the mushroom with yellow ochre. While the mushroom is still damp, add cadmium orange hue to the base of the mushroom cap and tips of the ears.

6. Add shadows and other details with burnt umber and then turquoise:

— While the cap is still wet, add burnt umber to the bottom of the mushroom cap.

— Paint a light wash of turquoise on the bow.

— Add shadows to the bottoms of the tiny mushrooms, as well as the body of the cat.

— Then add turquoise shadow lines along the underside of the mushroom cap and bottom edge of the top of the cap.

7. Build up the final details by layering more turquoise on the cat's bow. With emerald, paint the grass.

8. Outline your painting in ink.

SNAILGUS

SUPPLIES

Fine round brush
Medium round brush
Pen to outline

COLORS

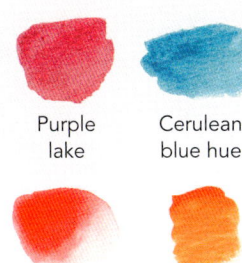
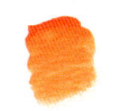

Purple lake	Cerulean blue hue	Yellow ochre	Cadmium yellow hue
Cadmium red deep hue	Cadmium orange hue	Emerald	

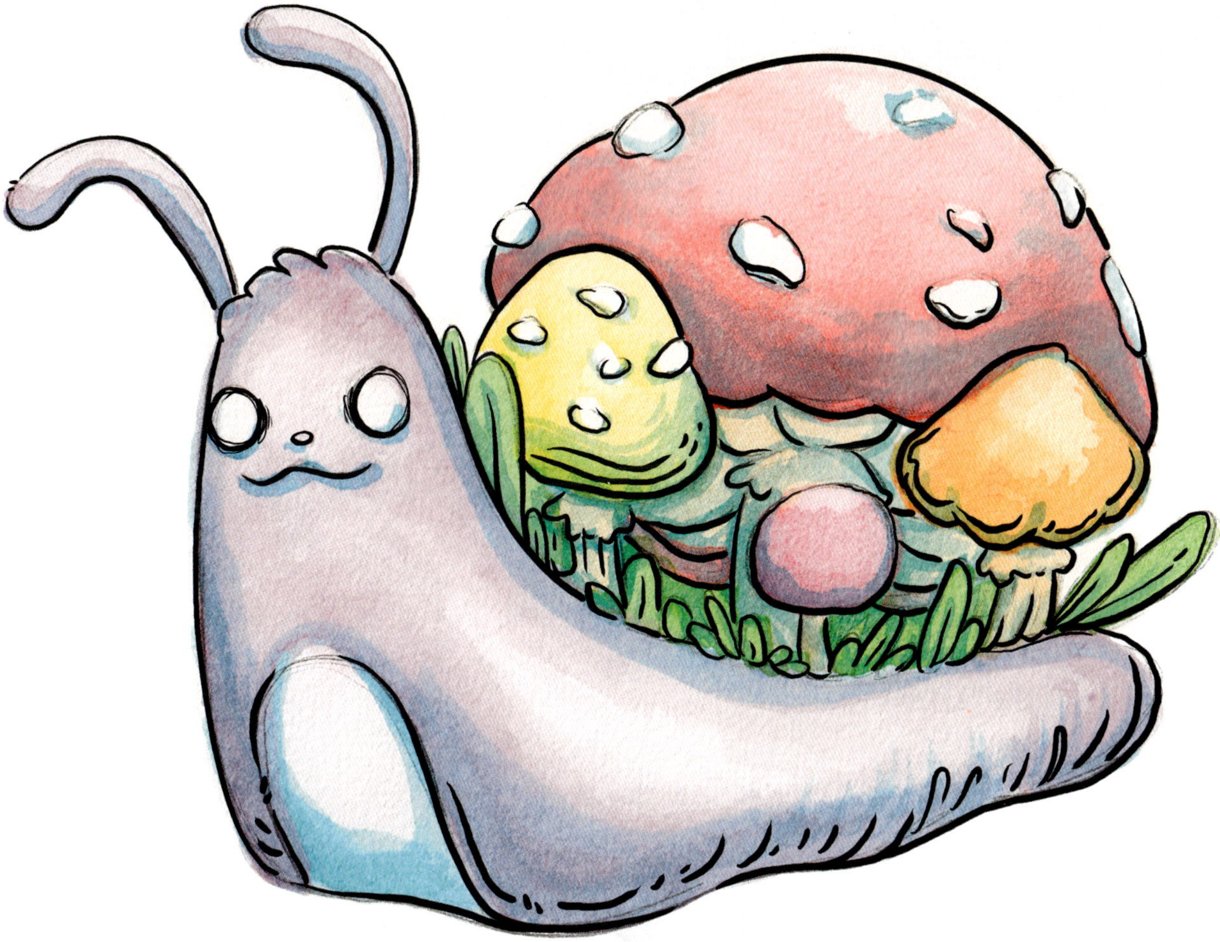

1

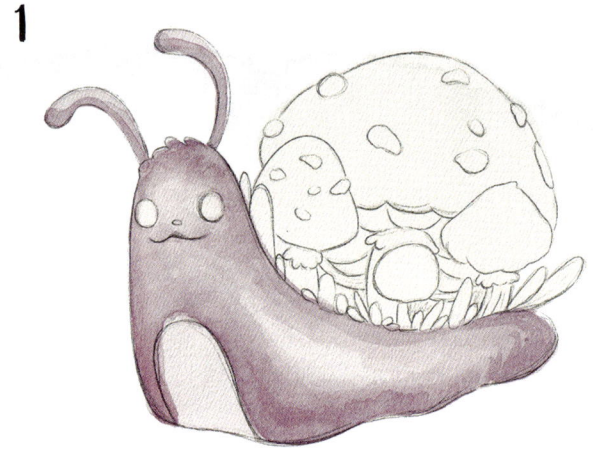

2

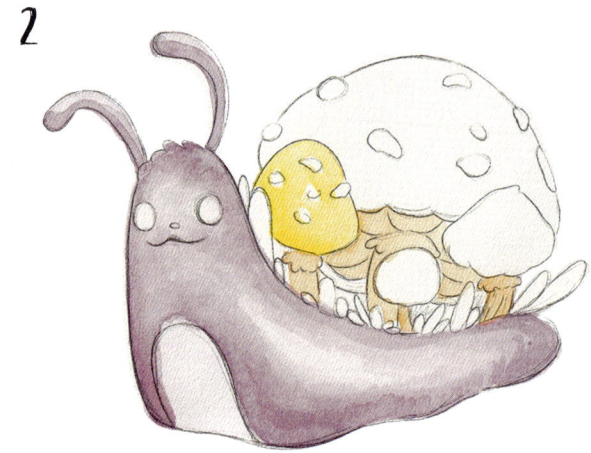

3

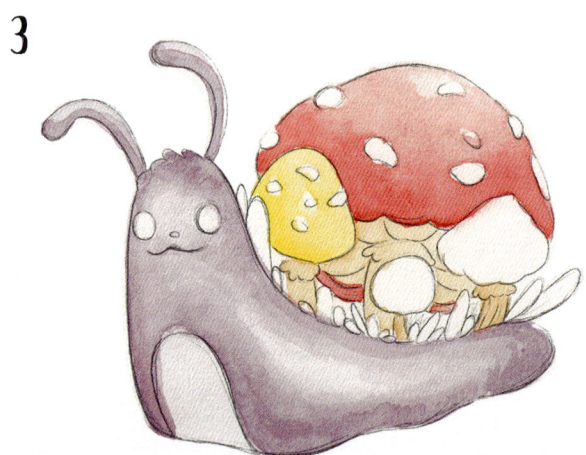

4

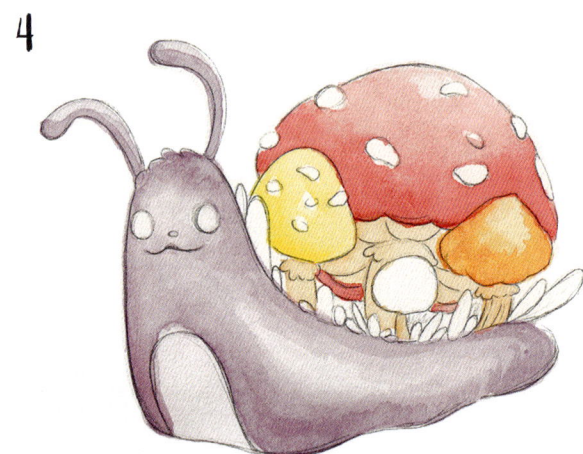

1. Mix equal parts purple lake and cerulean blue hue to create a light purple-gray shade. Using a medium round brush, paint a light wash on the snail's body, avoiding the stomach area and eyes. Allow to dry. Once dried, add a thicker layer of the color mix along the snail's body leaving a lighter area along the center of the side body. Keep doing this to build up contrast.

2. Using a fine round brush, add a wash of yellow ochre to the underside and stems of the largest mushroom. Allow to dry. Apply cadmium yellow hue to the medium mushroom on the left and let dry.

3. Using the wet-on-wet technique, apply water to the top of the largest mushroom. Avoid the white spots. Add cadmium red deep hue to the bottom of the mushroom and paint up.

4. For the medium mushroom on the right, paint a wash of cadmium orange hue. Wait until partially dry, then add a thicker coat of paint to the bottom and paint midway up the mushroom.

5

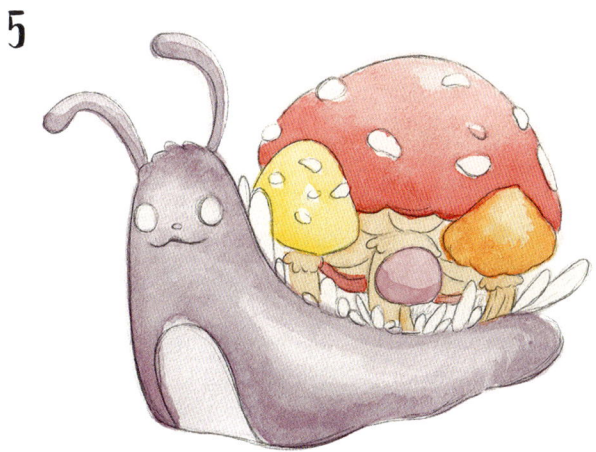

6

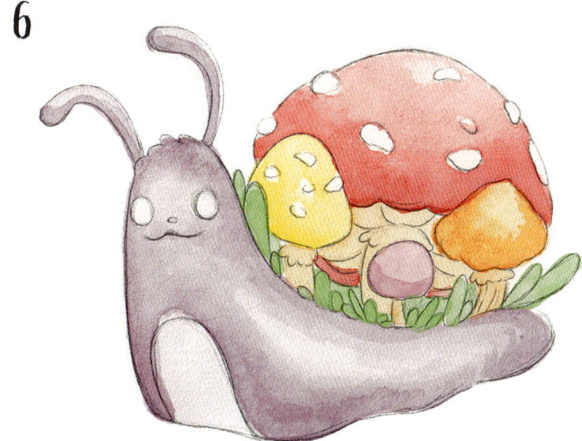

7

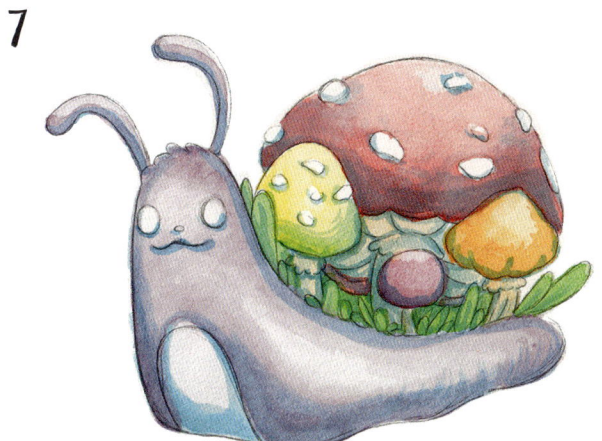

8

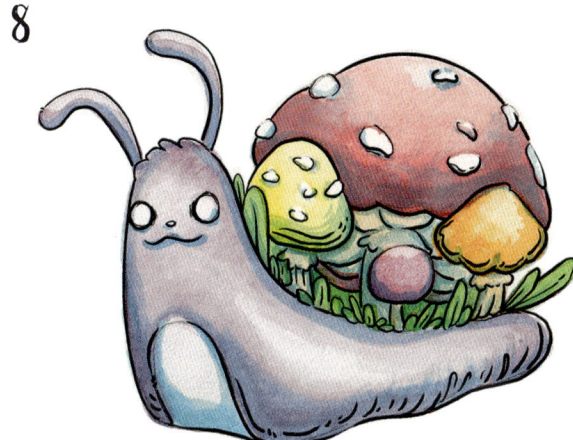

5. Paint the smallest mushroom with purple lake. Allow to dry. Then, add a shadow layer of purple lake along the bottom edge of the cap.

6. With a clean, fine round brush, paint with grass using emerald.

7. Add shadows with cerulean blue hue:

   — Add a strong shadow at the base of the snail's stomach.

   — Subtly outline the underside of the eyes, along the mouth, and the top of the body where the grass meets the snail.

   — Paint fine shadow lines on the underside of the largest mushroom cap and around the white spots.

8. Ink your painting.

SKULLOWERS

SUPPLIES

Fine round brush
Medium round brush
Pen to outline

COLORS

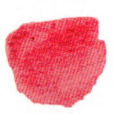

Yellow ochre

Purple lake

Permanent rose

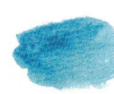

Cadmium yellow hue

Emerald

Cerulean blue hue

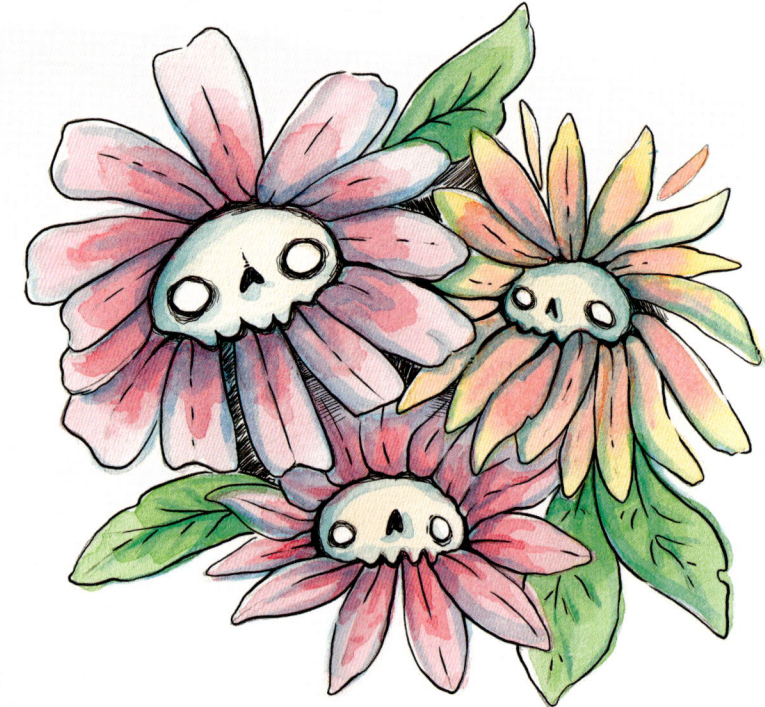

1

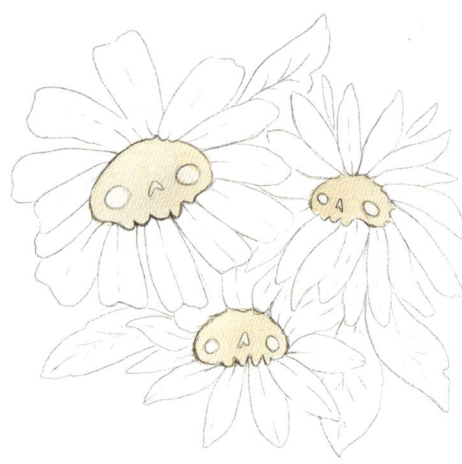

2

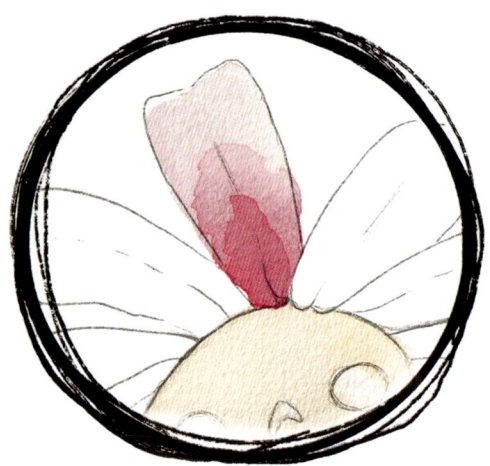

1. Using yellow ochre, lightly wash the skulls of the flower, and let dry.

2. For the first flower, mix even parts purple lake and permanent rose together. Using more water than color, use this mixture to paint one of the petals of the first flower. Let that petal partially dry, and then add a thicker layer of the paint mixture to the base of the flower and paint outward, stopping halfway to the flower's edge. Let partially dry before adding another layer of paint to the base of the flower, again painting outward, and stopping at a quarter way to the flower's edge.

3

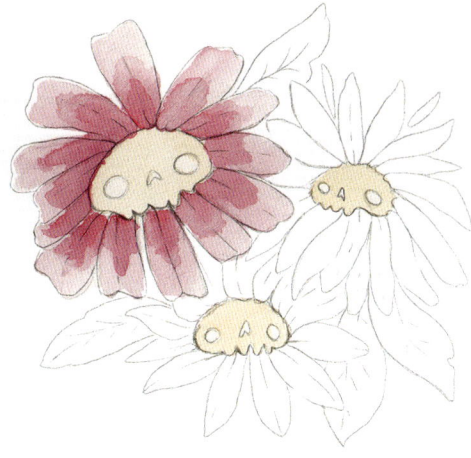

4

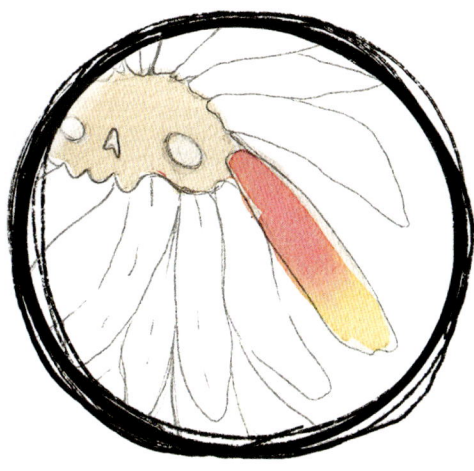

5

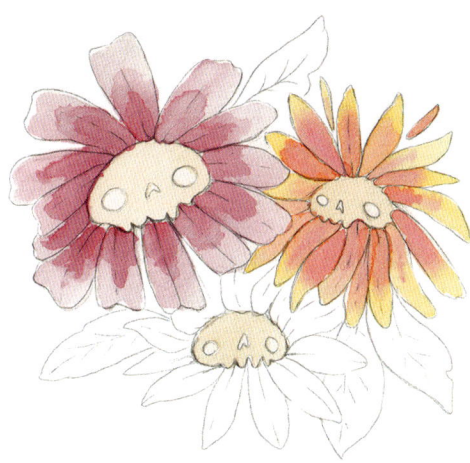

6

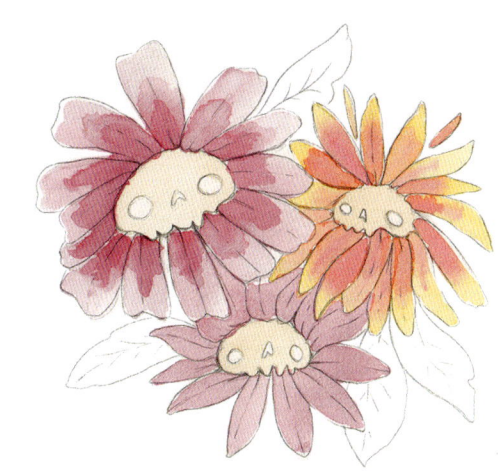

3. Use this same technique to paint the rest of the first flower's petals. Let each flower petal fully dry before moving on to the next petal. This way the flower petals don't bleed together.

4. For this step you have to act quickly, so make sure your paints are ready—you'll need cadmium yellow hue, as well as the mixture from the previous steps. Using cadmium yellow hue, paint one of the petals of the second flower. Before it dries, quickly take the purple lake and permanent rose mixture and paint the petal starting in the middle, painting toward the skull. Let dry.

5. Repeat this step to paint the rest of the flower petals, allowing each petal to dry before moving to the next so the petals don't bleed together.

6. Using permanent rose, lightly paint the third flower and let dry.

7

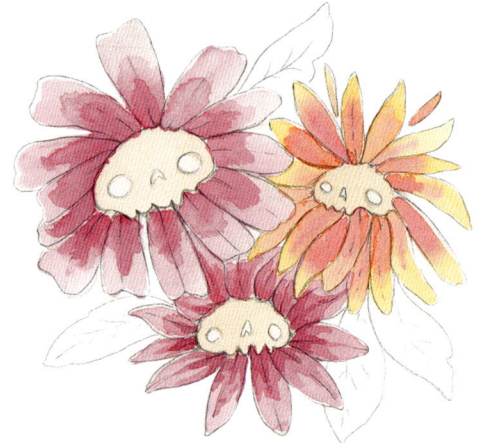

8

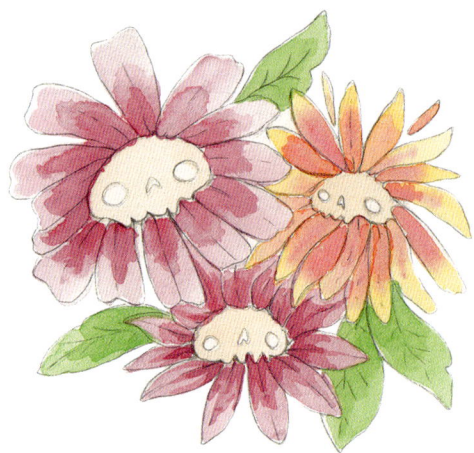

9

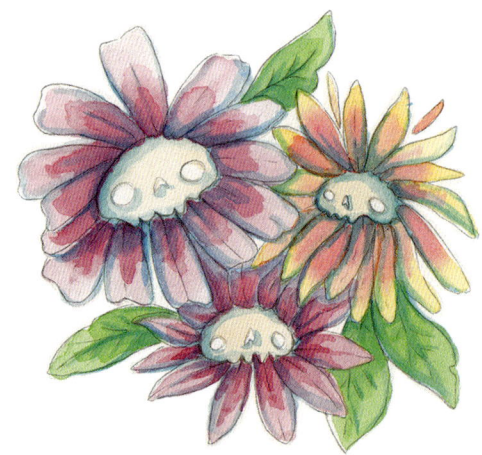

10

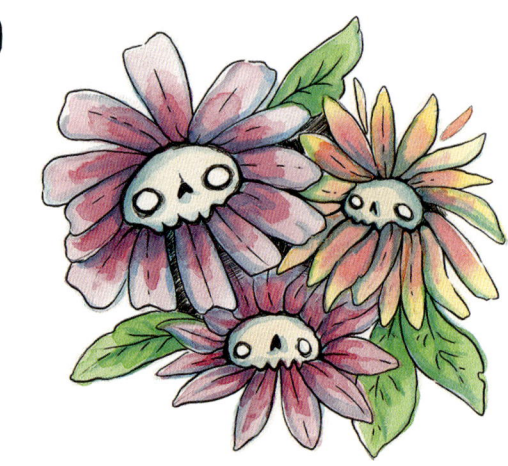

7. Using less water, paint permanent rose on the base of the petals on the third flower. Paint outward, stopping before you reach the tip of the petal. Repeat, letting the paint dry in between, to build up layers and contrast on the flower.

8. Mix emerald and cadmium yellow hue together. Use this mixture to lightly wash the leaves of the flowers, and let dry. Using less water and more paint, add another layer of the green mixture, painting the base of the leaves halfway to the leaf edges.

9. Paint a light wash of cerulean blue hue on the flowers for shadows. Paint along the lines of the flowers and let dry. Using less water and more of the cerulean blue hue paint, apply more shadows to the flowers.

10. Ink the outline of your painting.

CATUS

SUPPLIES

Fine round brush
Medium round brush
Pen to outline

COLORS

 Emerald

 Cadmium yellow hue

 Cadmium orange hue

 Permanent rose

 Burnt sienna

 Yellow ochre

 Cerulean blue hue

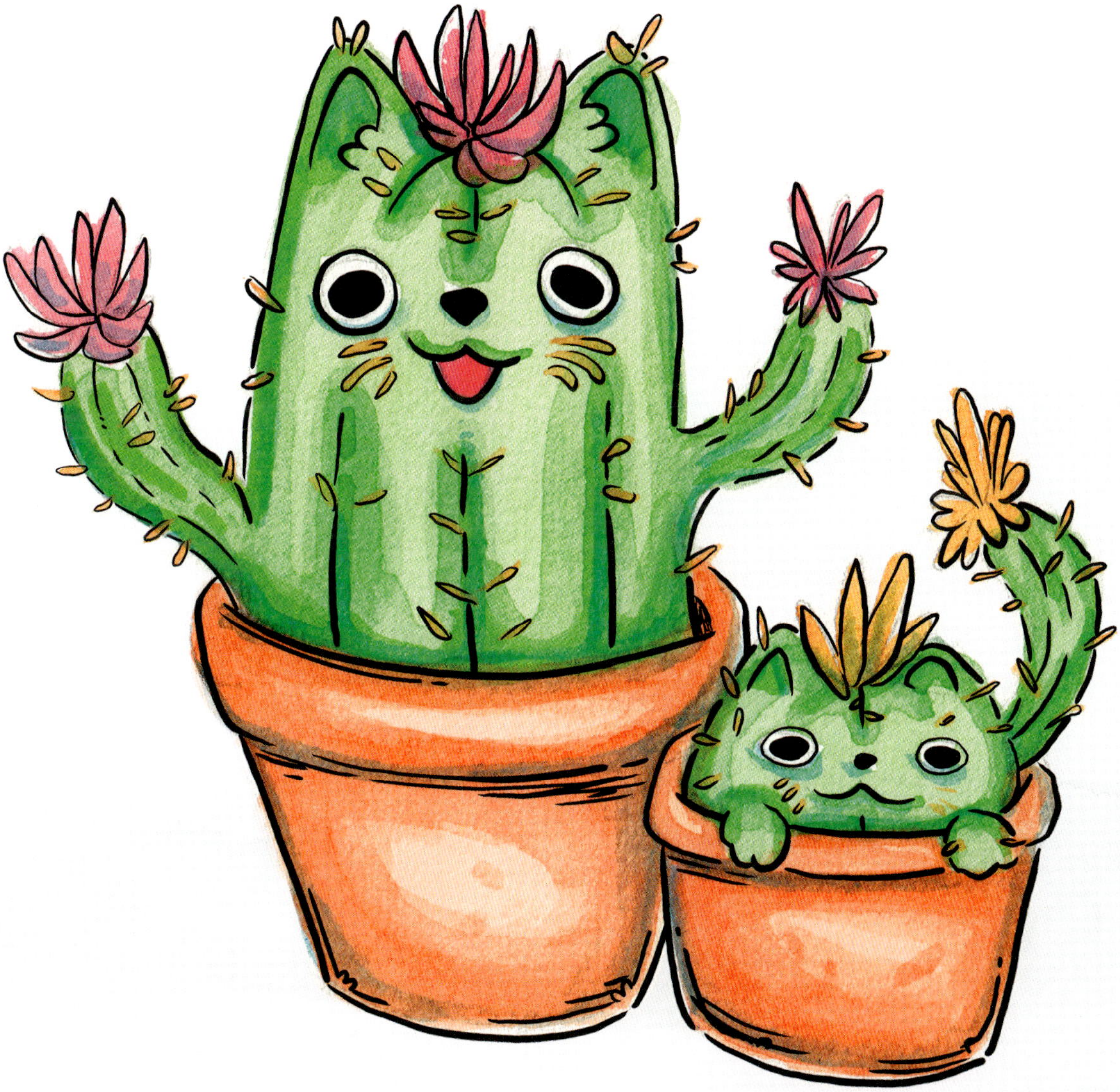

1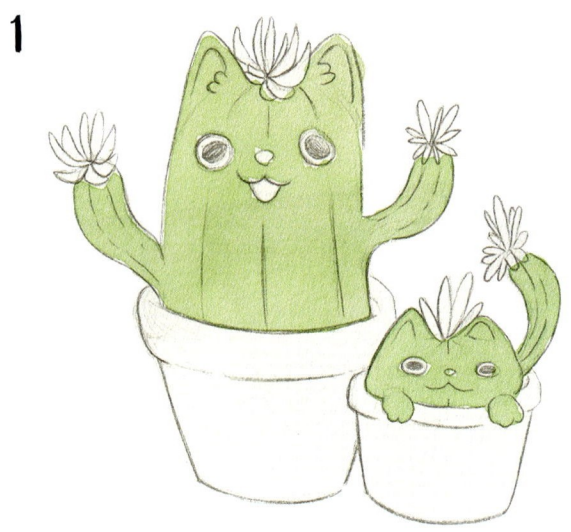

2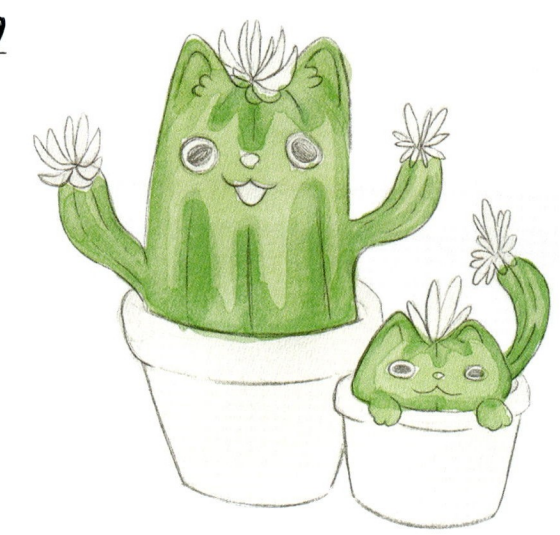

3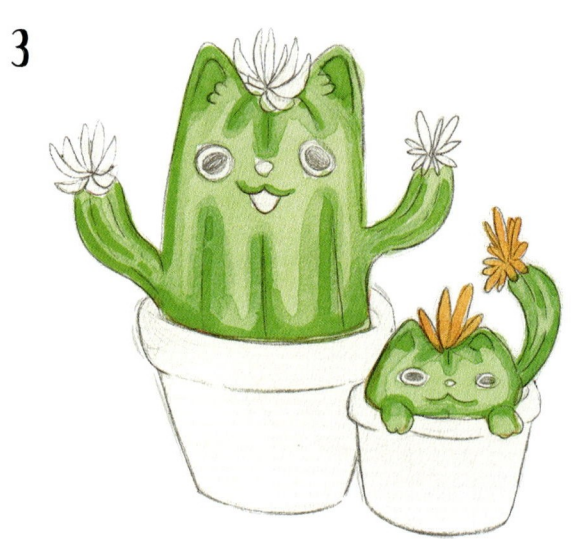

4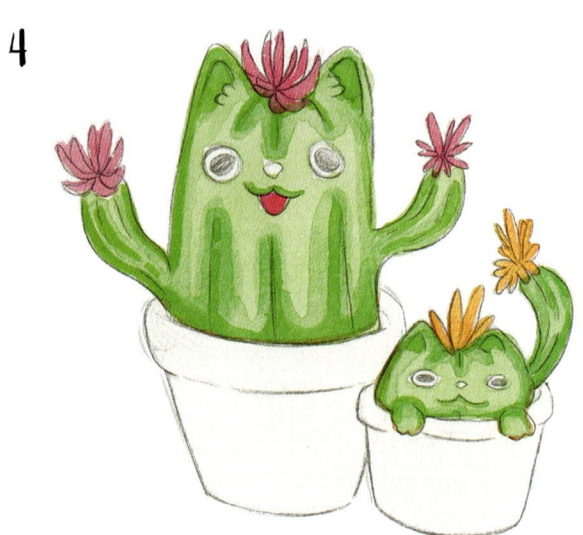

1. Mix emerald and cadmium yellow hue and paint a wash over the bodies of the cat cacti. Let dry.

2. Using less water and more paint, apply the mixture around the lines on the cat cacti.

3. Using even less water, paint the mixture again on the outlines of the cat cacti. Then use cadmium orange hue to paint the flowers of the small cat.

4. Apply permanent rose to the flowers and mouth of the second cat.

5

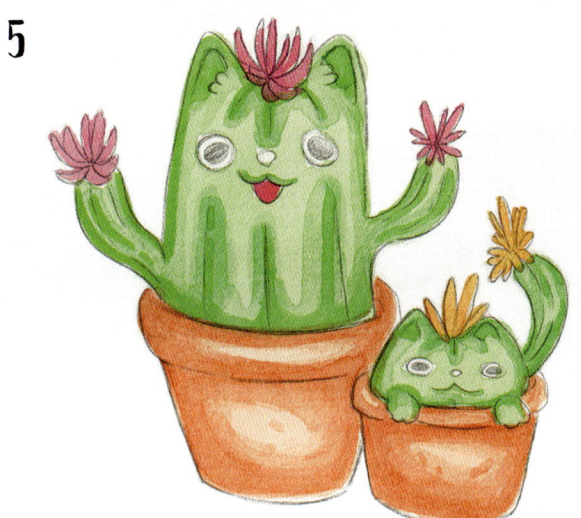

6

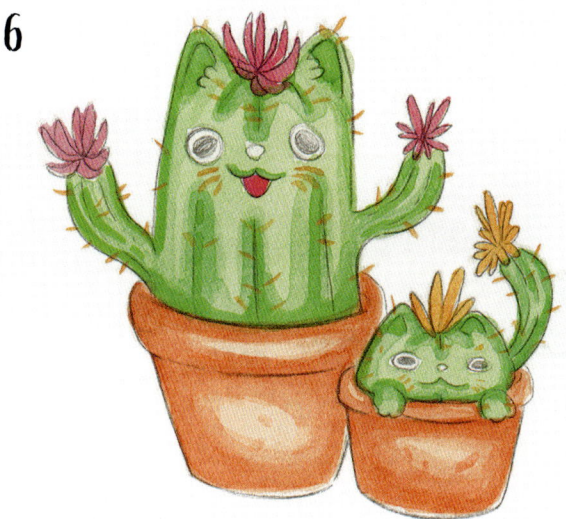

7

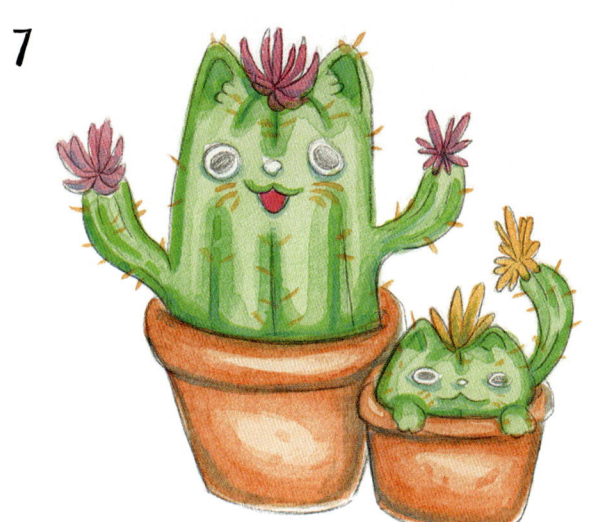

8

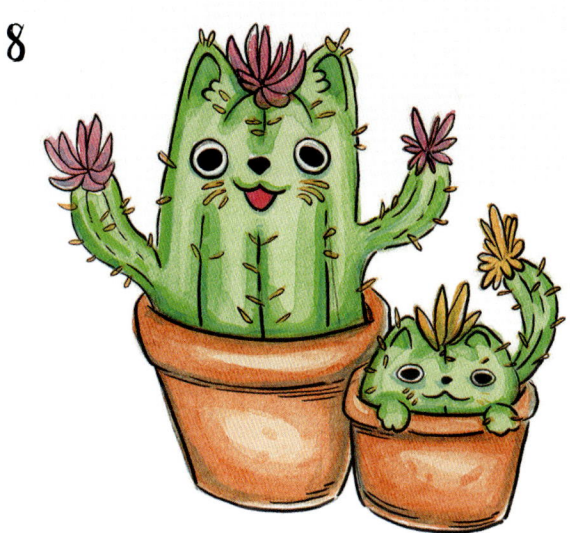

5. Paint a wash of burnt sienna on the pots and let dry. Use a thicker mixture of burnt sienna around the outlines of the pots, and keep adding layers until you're satisfied with the values. Leave some lighter areas at the front of the pots to show reflection.

6. Use a thick mixture of yellow ochre to paint the spikes of the cactus randomly.

7. Use a light mixture of cerulean blue hue to paint the shadows.

8. Ink the outline of your catus!

LILY OF DEATH VALLEY

SUPPLIES

Fine round brush
Medium round brush
Pen to outline

COLORS

Cadmium
yellow hue
Emerald
Turquoise

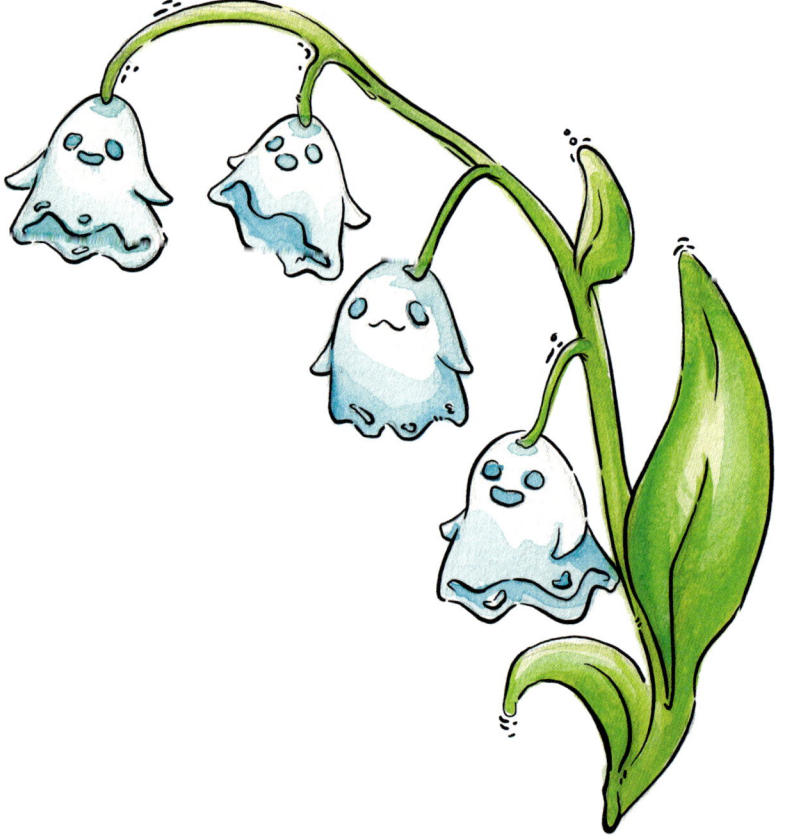

1. This project will just be a fun, simple exercise! Since the flowers are ghosts, we'll simply use the white of the paper and add some shading. Start by mixing cadmium yellow hue and emerald together. Paint a light wash on the stem and leaves and let dry.

2. Using more of the mixture and less water, add another layer of the paint to the leaves and stem.

3. Continue to add thicker layers of paint on parts of the leaves to build up contrast and create dimension.

4. Add turquoise paint to the first ghost, let dry, and add more turquoise to build up layers.

5. Repeat step 4 to paint the remaining ghosts.

6. Ink the outline of your painting

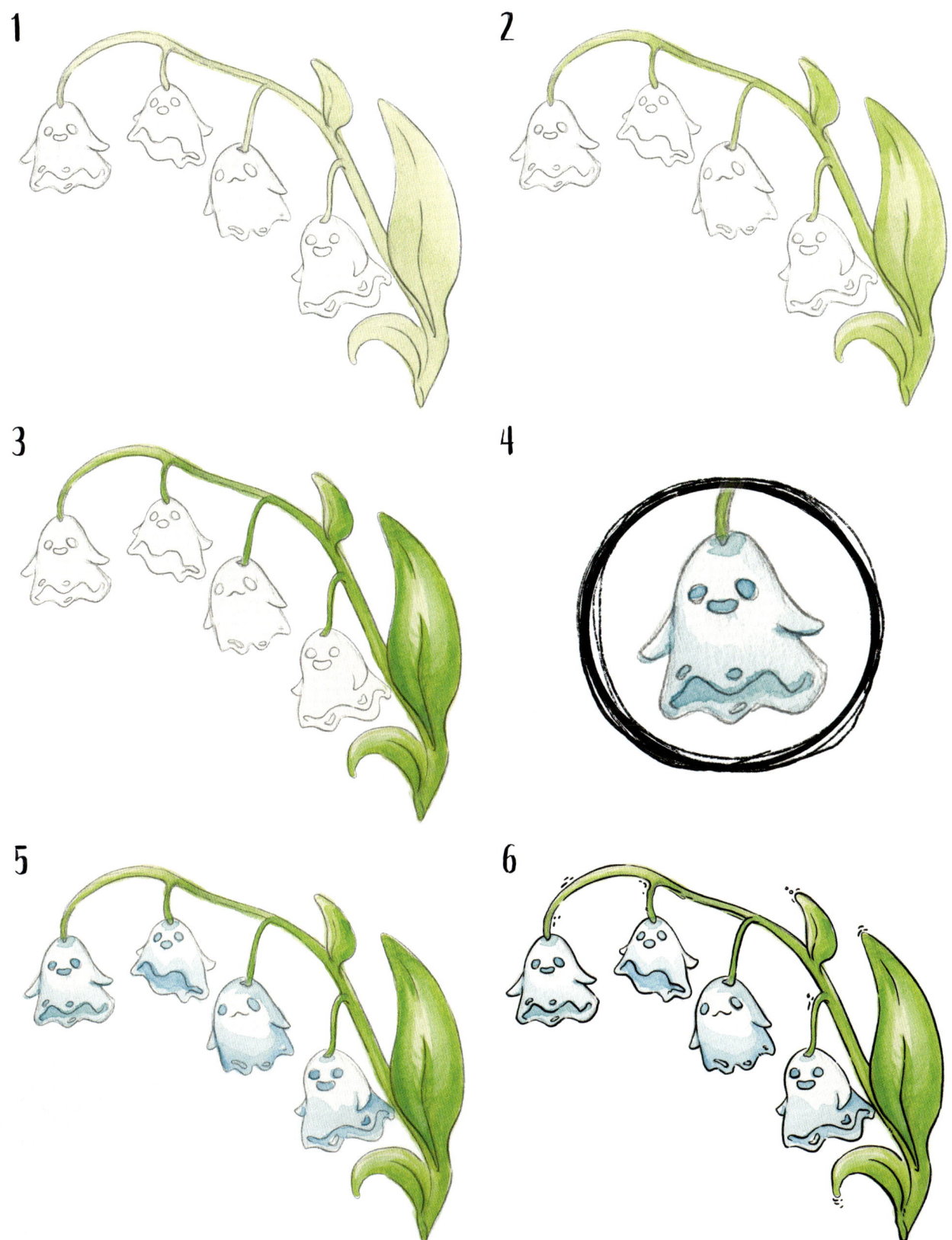

VENUS FLYTRAP

SUPPLIES

Fine round brush
Medium round brush
Pen to outline

COLORS

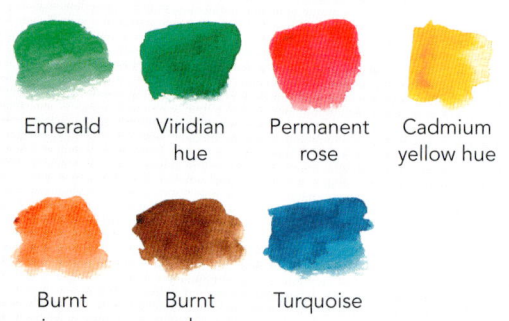

Emerald

Viridian
hue

Permanent
rose

Cadmium
yellow hue

Burnt
sienna

Burnt
umber

Turquoise

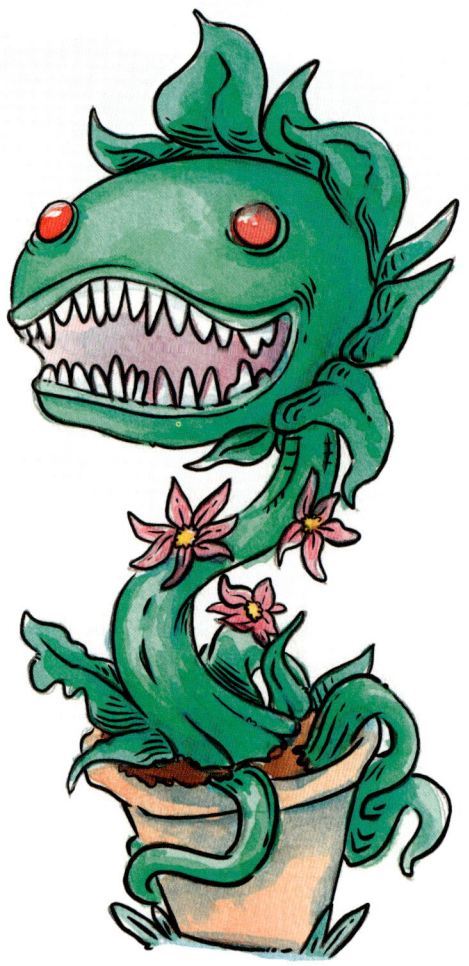

1. Start by painting a light wash of emerald on the body of the plant and let dry. Once dry, add a second darker layer of emerald, leaving some of the previous layer exposed to provide highlights.

2. Next, paint a medium wash of viridian hue on the leaves of the plant.

3. Add a thicker layer of viridian to the leaves of the plant. Start from the base of each leaf and paint outward to create a gradient effect.

4. For the inside of the mouth, use permanent rose. Start from the inner side of the mouth and paint outward. Be careful to avoid the whites of the teeth. Use a smaller brush to paint the petals of the flowers. Once dry, use cadmium yellow hue to paint the centers of the flowers. Fill the pot with a light wash of burnt sienna.

5. For the soil, paint a dark layer of burnt umber using a smaller brush. Use your small brush to paint the eyes permanent rose. Leave a small white spot in each eye for highlights. For the shadows, paint a light layer of turquoise.

6. Ink in your painting.

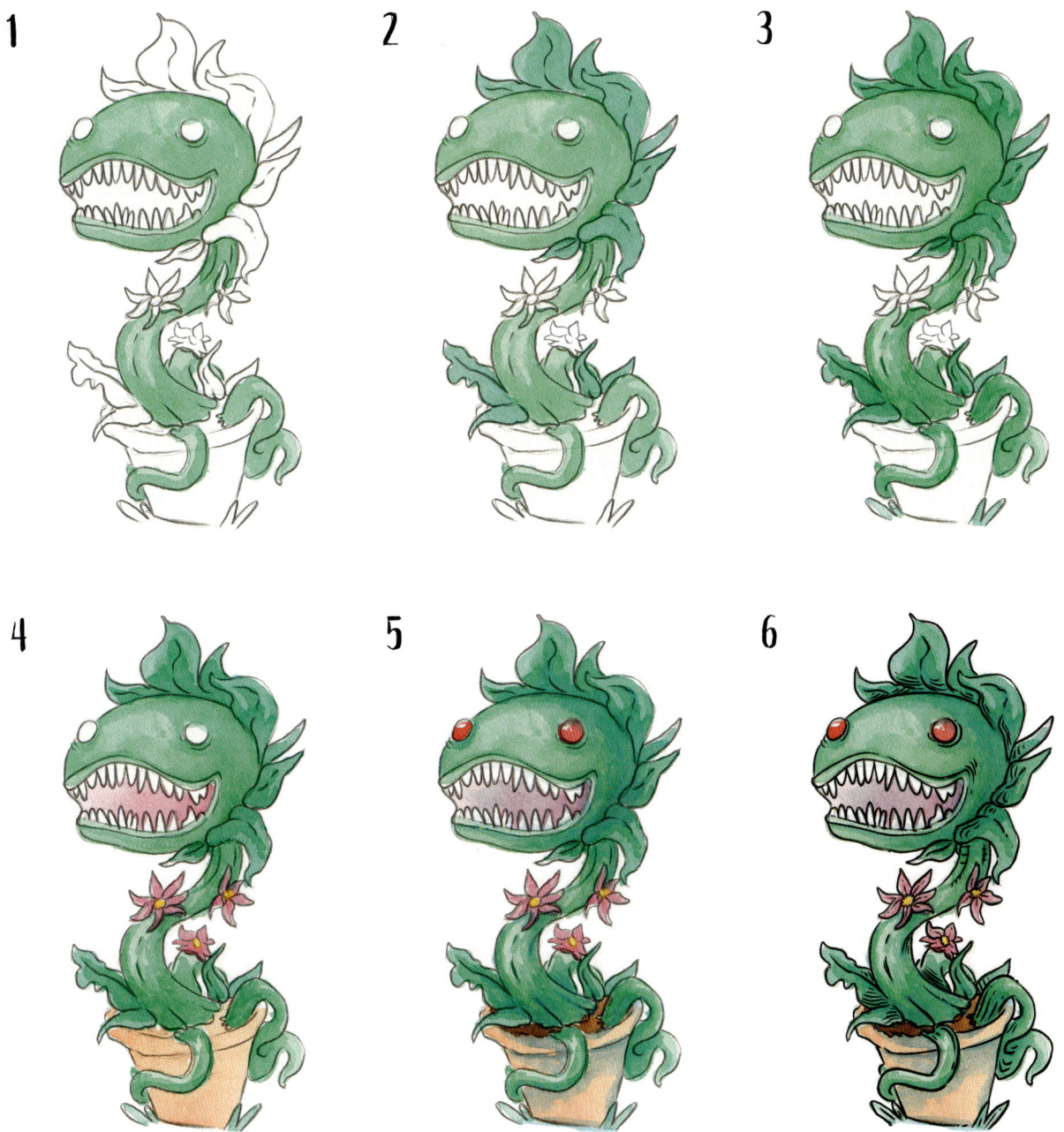

1 **2** **3**

4 **5** **6**

LEAF SPRITES

SUPPLIES

Fine round brush
Medium round brush
Pen to outline and fill bodies
White pen for highlights

COLORS

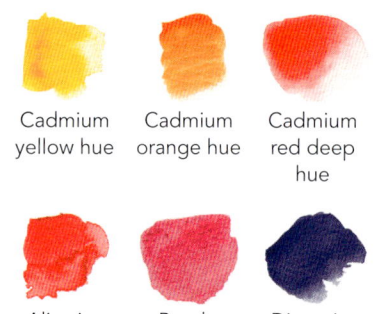

Cadmium yellow hue   Cadmium orange hue   Cadmium red deep hue

Alizarin crimson hue   Purple lake   Dioxazine purple

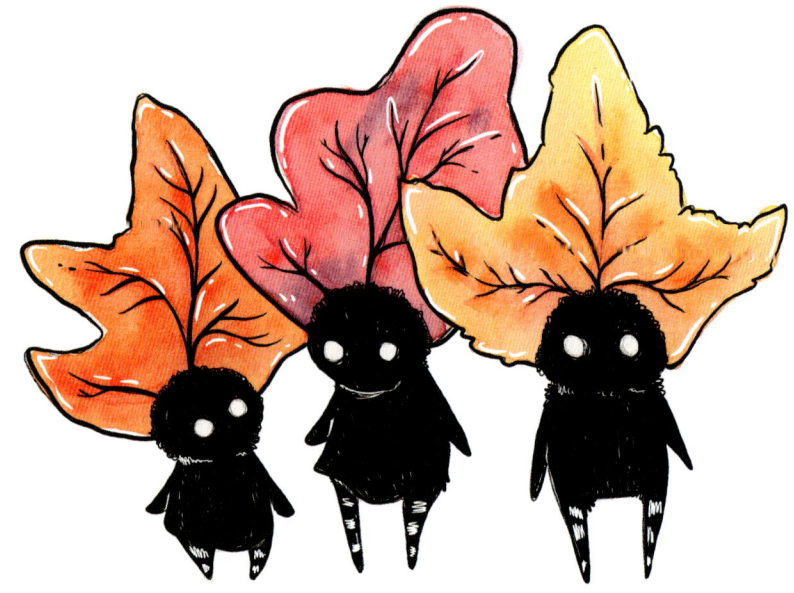

1. Paint the first leaf cadmium yellow hue. While the paint is wet, load your brush up with cadmium orange hue and blot it around the yellow leaf. Repeat with cadmium red deep hue. Then let dry.

2. Paint the second leaf cadmium orange hue and, while still wet, blot the colors alizarin crimson hue and purple lake around the orange leaf. Let dry.

3. Paint the last leaf purple lake. While still wet, blot on alizarin crimson hue and dioxazine purple around the leaf. Then let dry.

4. Once all the leaves are dry, use dioxazine purple to paint shadows along the lines of the leaves.

5. Ink in the bodies of the leaves.

6. If you have a white pen (or white colored pencil), add some highlights to the veins of the leaves and bodies of the sprites. For the sprites, the lines are added along the chin line, where the arms meet the body, and striped stockings on the legs.

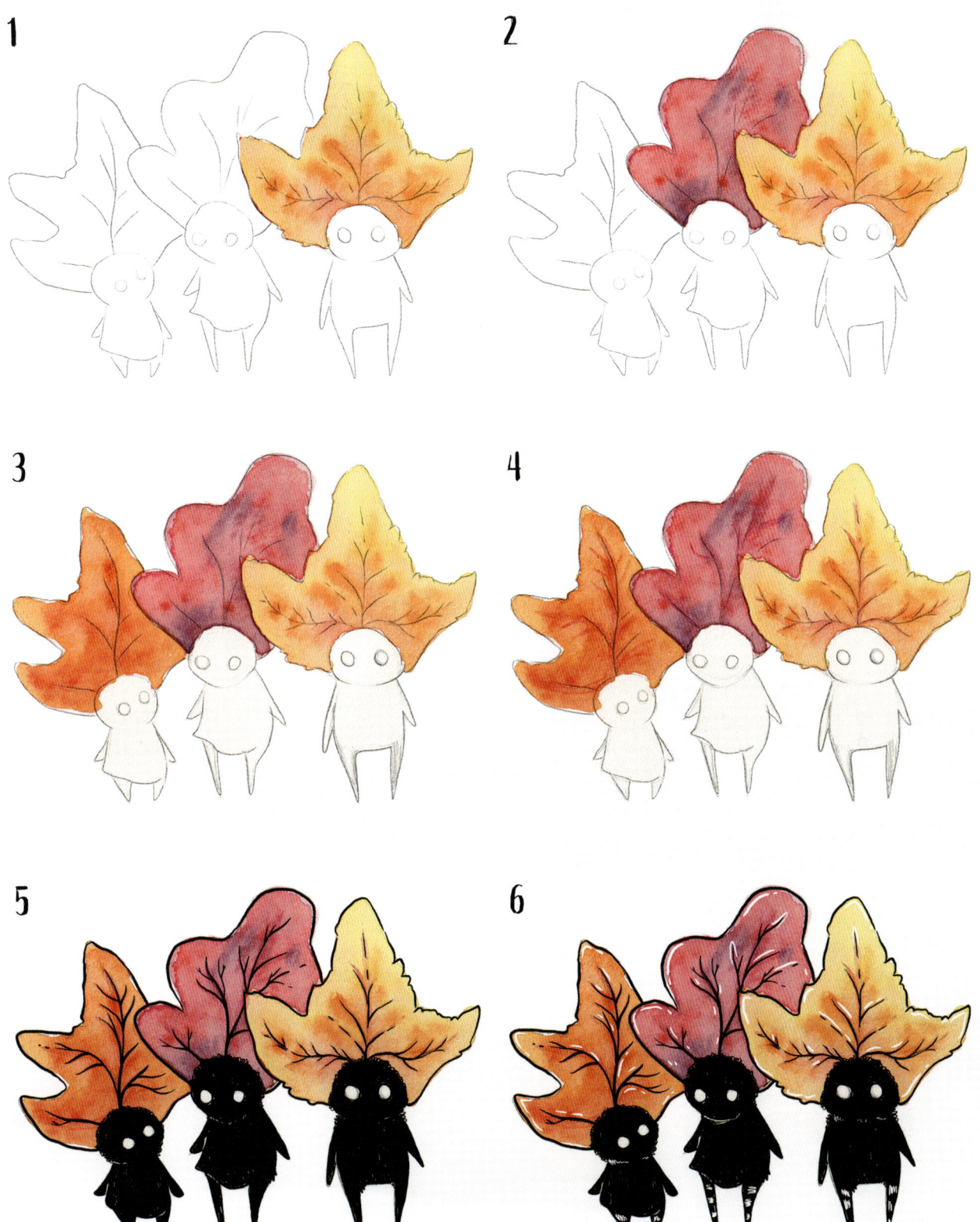

POPSICKLES

SUPPLIES

Fine round brush
Medium round brush
Pen to outline

COLORS

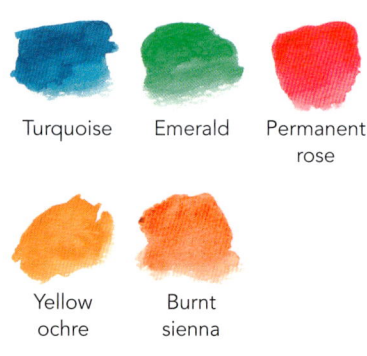

Turquoise   Emerald   Permanent
                        rose

Yellow   Burnt
ochre   sienna

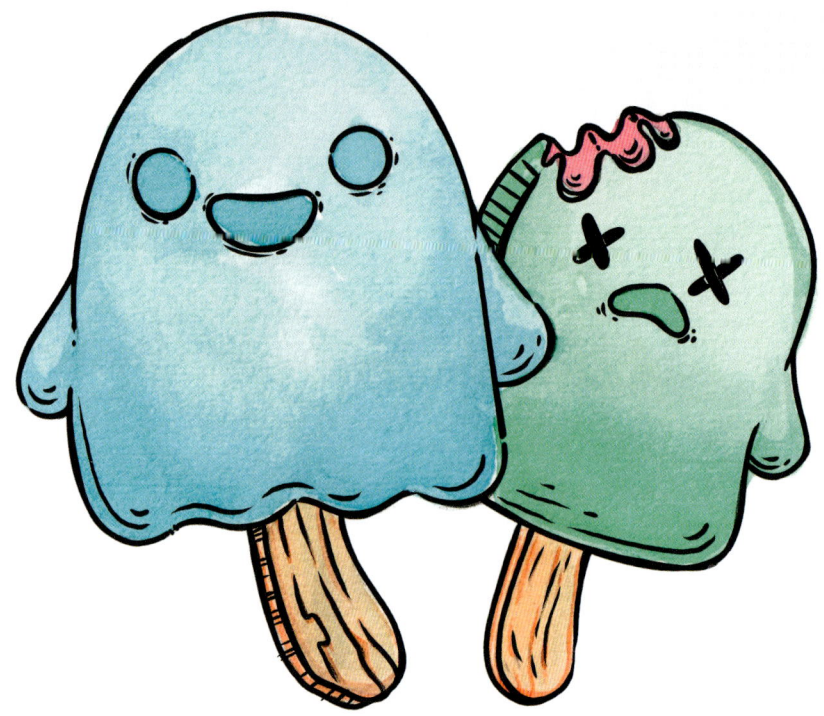

1. With a medium-size brush, paint a light wash of
   turquoise on the left ghost. Start on the outer
   edge of the body and paint inward, and let
   dry. Add a darker layer of paint on the bottom of
   the body and paint upward to add more shading
   to the ghost. Then add a darker layer of paint to
   the inside of the eyes and mouth.

2. Repeat step 1 for the second ghost, using
   emerald.

3. For the bite mark in the ice cream, paint with
   permanent rose.

4. Mix 50% yellow ochre with 50% burnt sienna
   and paint on a light layer on the sticks.

5. Use a small fine-tipped brush to paint burnt
   sienna on the lines on the popsicle sticks to add
   a wood-grain effect.

6. Outline your painting in ink.

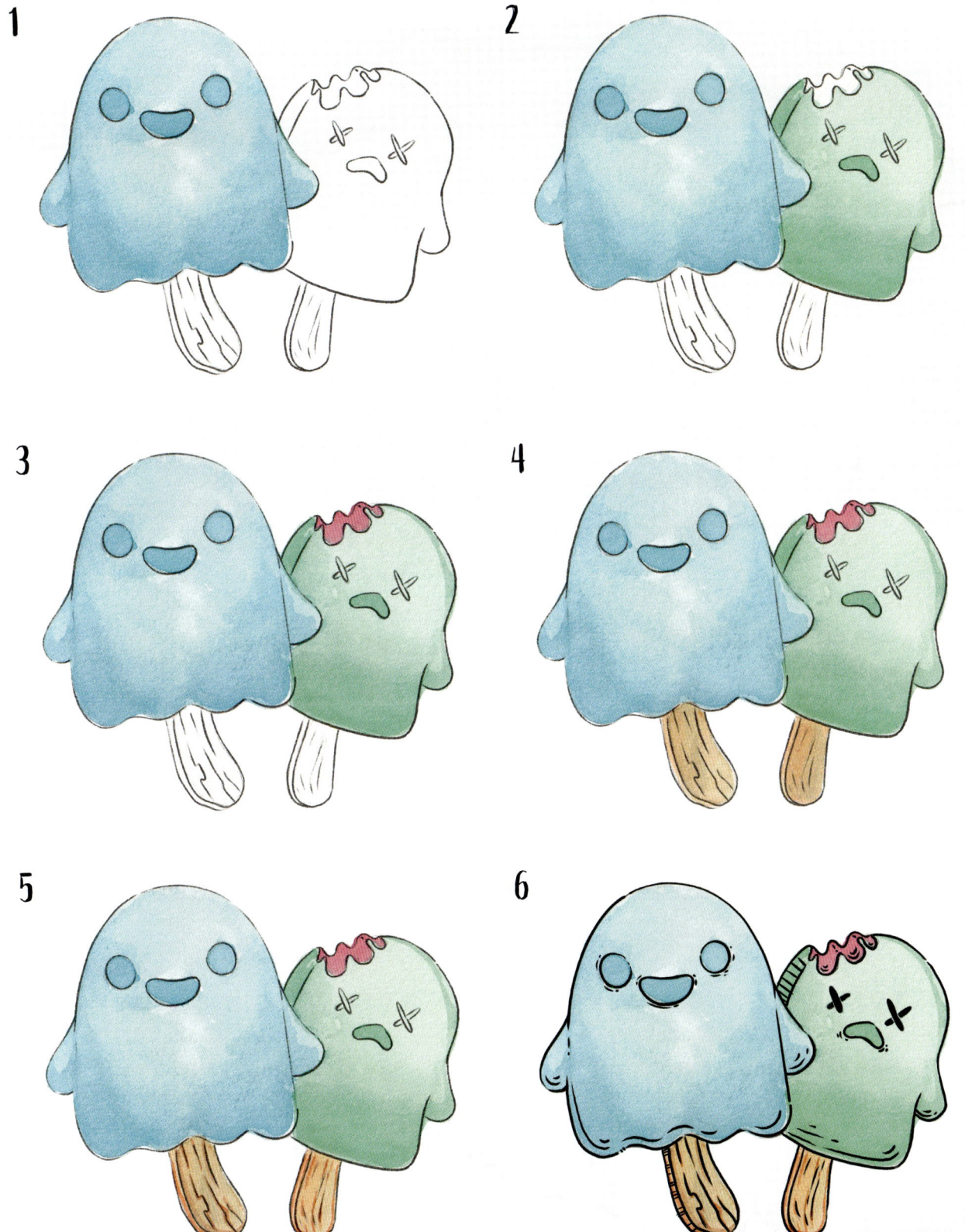

HOT DAWGS

SUPPLIES

Fine round brush
Medium round brush
Pen to outline

COLORS

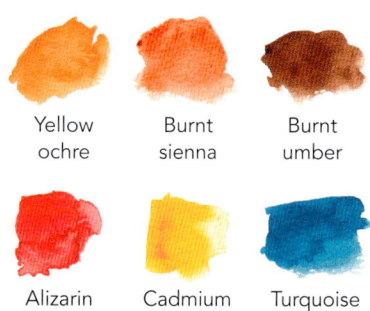

Yellow ochre

Burnt sienna

Burnt umber

Alizarin crimson hue

Cadmium yellow hue

Turquoise

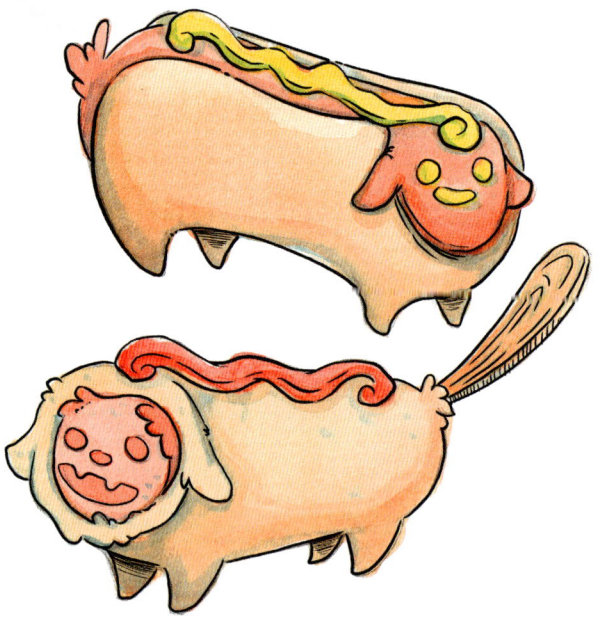

1

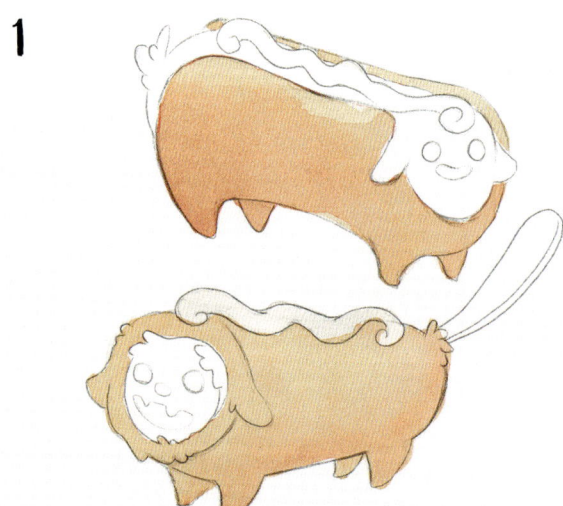

2

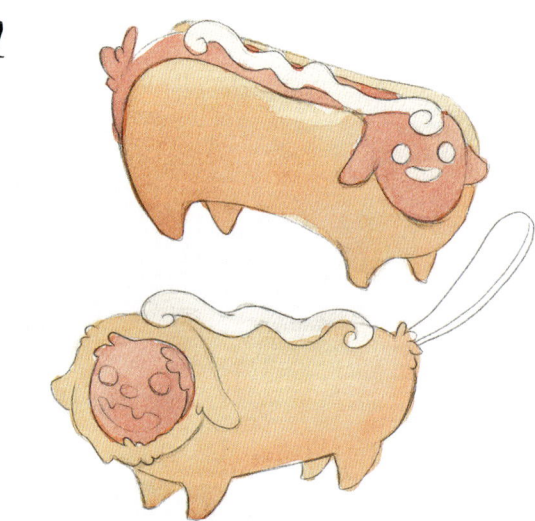

1. Paint a light wash of yellow ochre on the buns of the dogs. Don't let fully dry before moving to the next step. While the paint is still wet, add burnt sienna, starting at the bottom of the buns and painting halfway up. Then let fully dry.

2. Mix burnt umber and alizarin crimson hue together, and apply a light wash to the bodies of the dogs. Let fully dry.

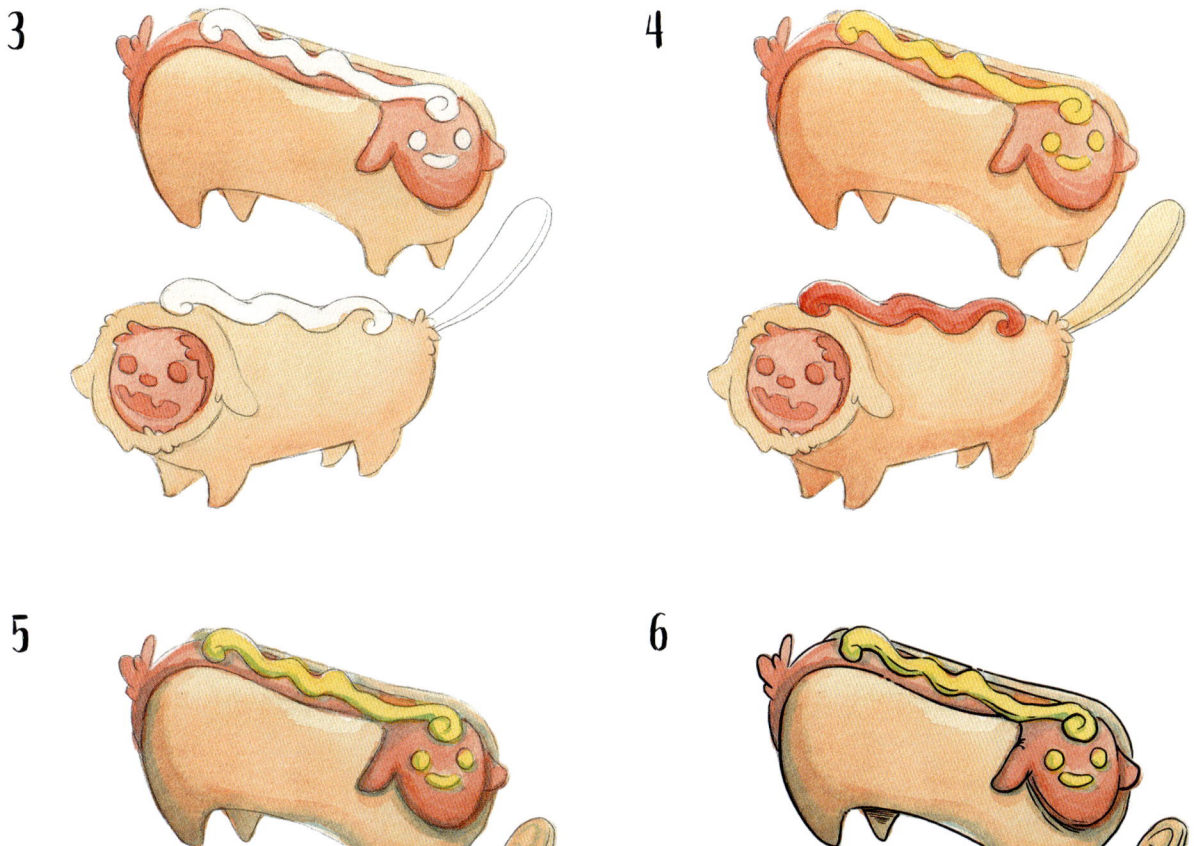

3. Using a thicker layer of the mixture from step 2, paint the details on the dogs' bodies, such as the face and outline.

4. Use cadmium yellow hue to paint the mustard on the first dog. Use alizarin crimson hue to paint the ketchup on the second dog.

5. Use a light wash of turquoise to paint some shading on the dogs. Not certain where to paint the shading? Start by painting along the outlines on the bottom of the dogs.

6. Outline your painting in ink.

SCARY CHERRY PIE

SUPPLIES

Fine round brush
Medium round brush
Pen to outline

COLORS

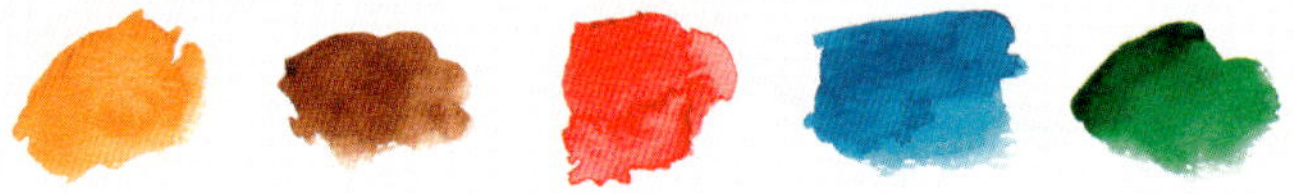

| Yellow ochre | Burnt umber | Alizarin crimson hue | Turquoise | Hooker's green |

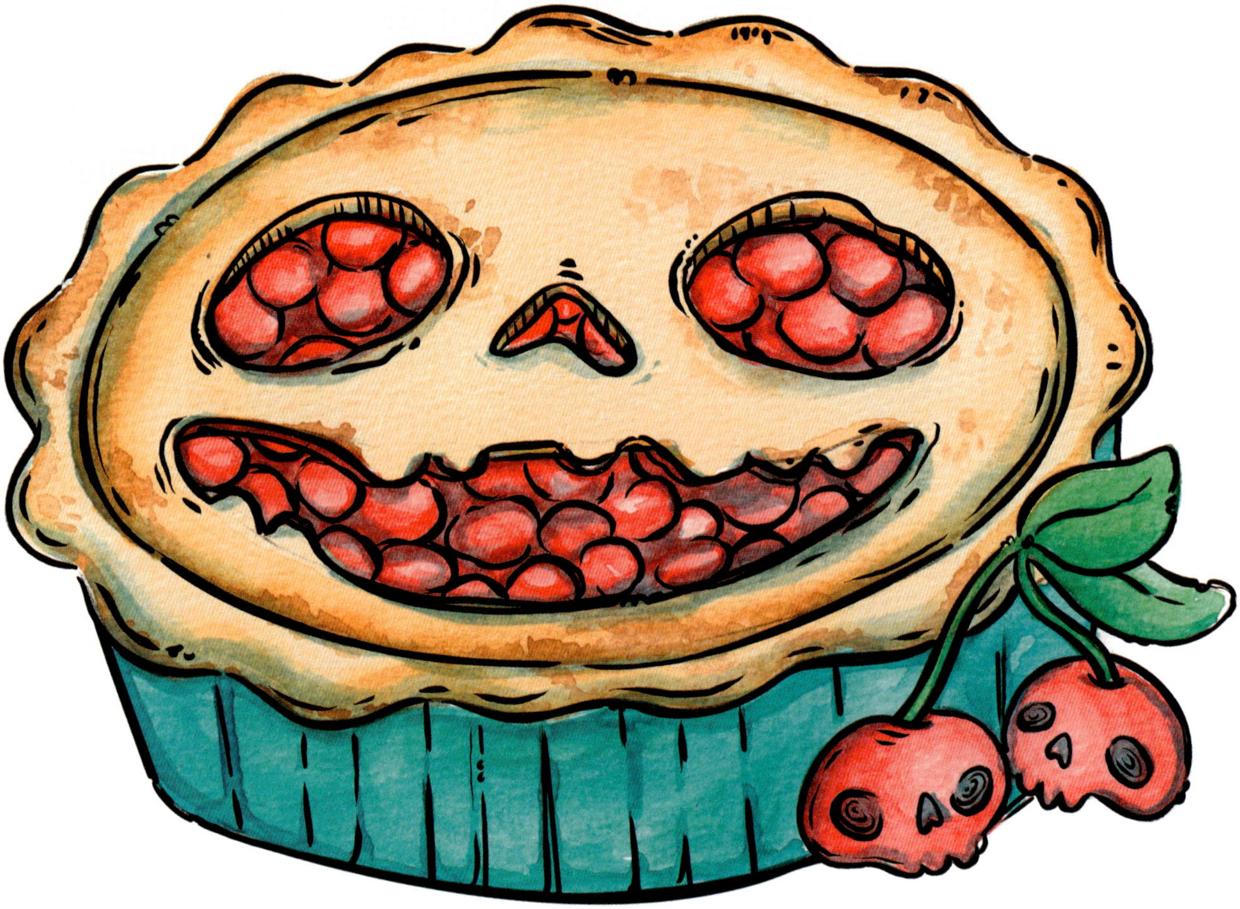

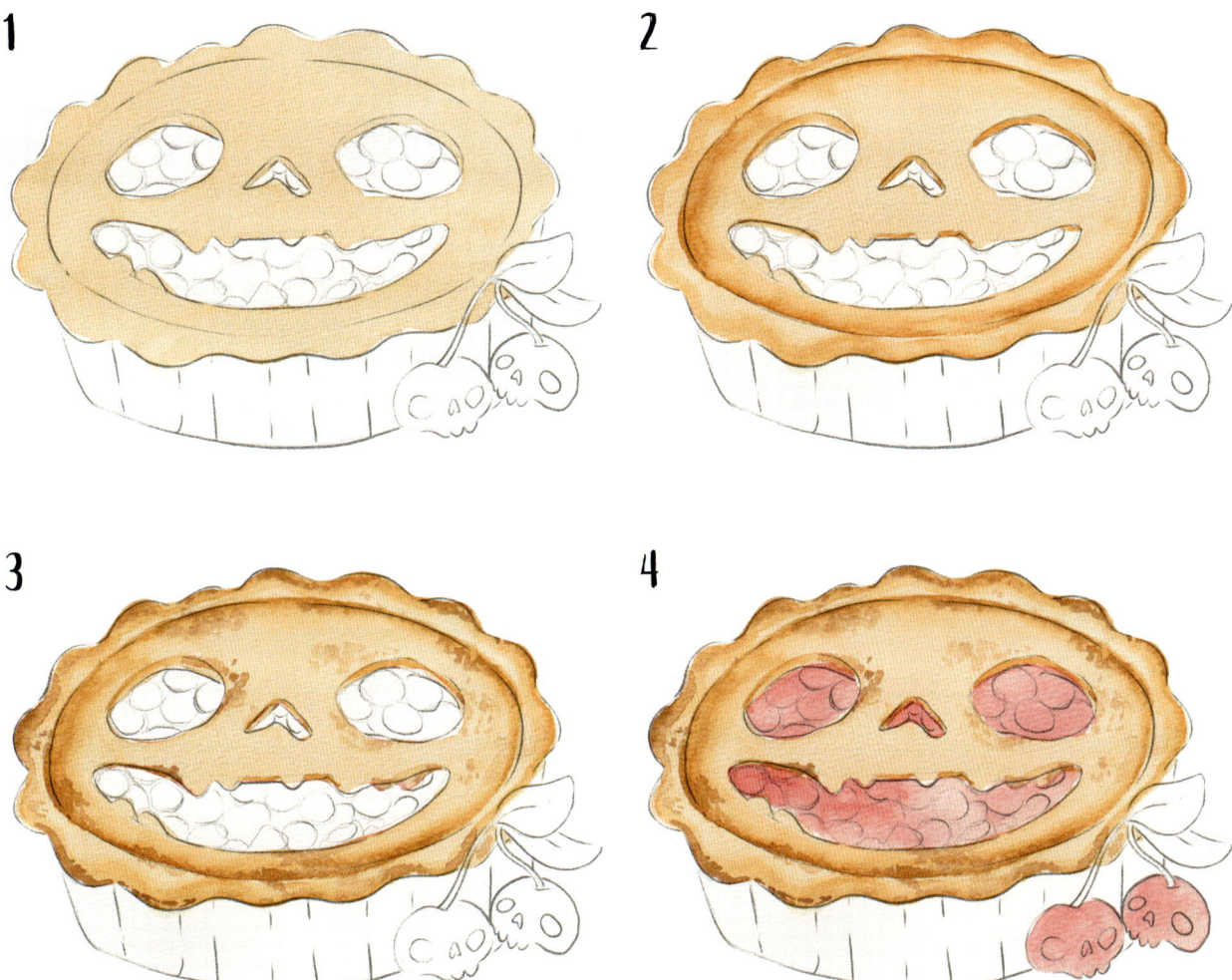

1. Create a mix with 40% yellow ochre and 60% burnt umber. Apply a light wash with a medium round brush on the pie crust and let dry.

2. Using this same mixture, apply a darker layer of paint around the outlines to give the appearance that the pie is cooked and crisp. With a finer round brush, paint the inside edge of the eyes, mouth, and nose.

3. Mix a medium amount of burnt umber with water and apply another darker layer with the small brush around the outlines to resemble burnt edges. Speckle some of the color around the pie to give it some texture.

4. Use a medium-size brush to apply a light wash of alizarin crimson hue to the cherries inside of the pie, as well as the small skull cherries. Let dry.

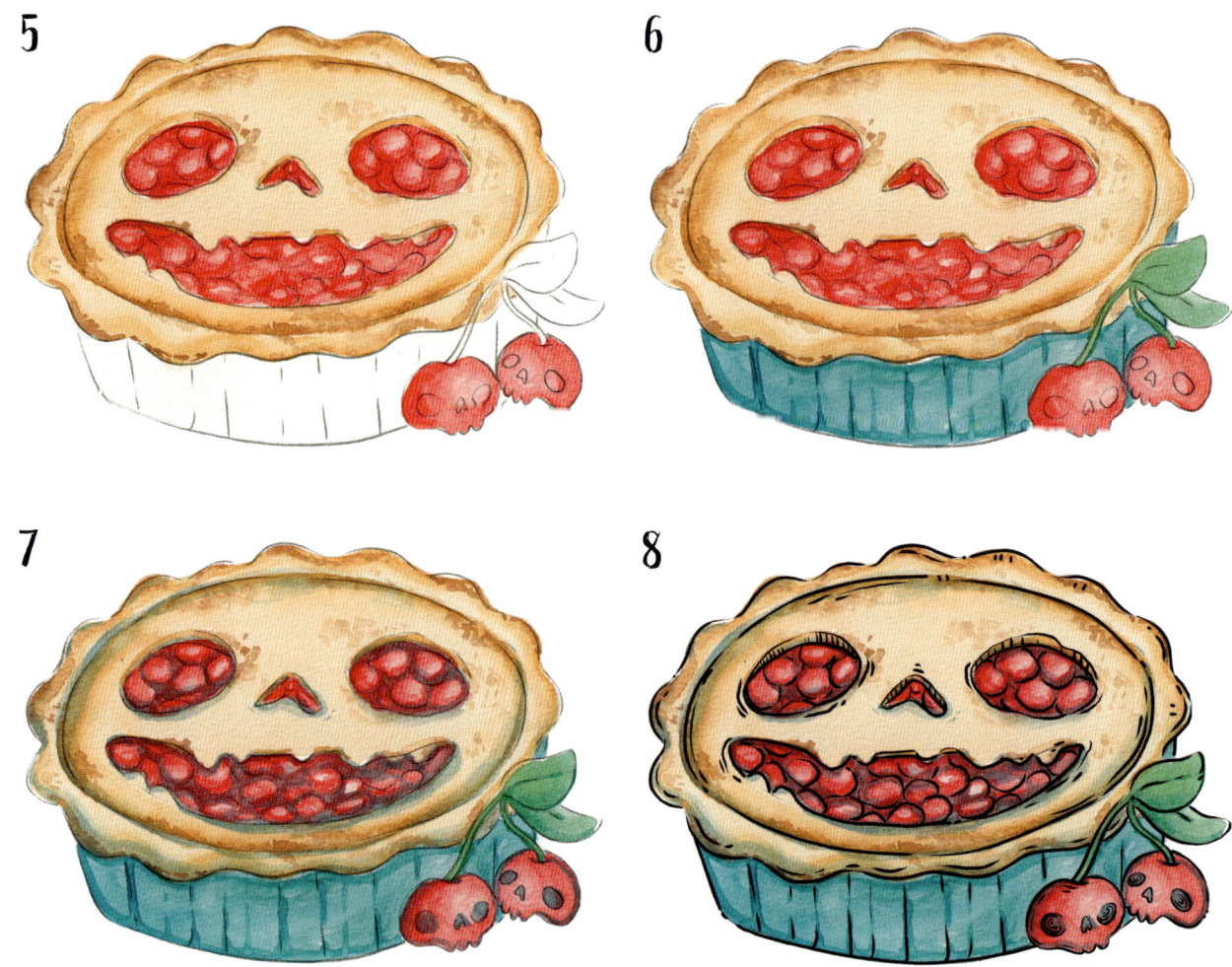

5. Using a smaller brush, apply a darker layer of alizarin crimson hue to the cherries. Paint around the circles (cherries) and paint inward, leaving the inner circles lighter to suggest highlights. Do this for the skull cherries as well. Let dry and repeat the process to build up the values.

6. For the pie pan, mix 70% turquoise with 30% yellow ochre and paint on a dark wash using a medium-size brush. Let dry. Using the same mixture, use a fine-tipped brush (such as 4) to paint the lines of the pan. For the skull cherry leaves and stems, apply a medium wash of Hooker's green and let dry.

7. For the shadows, mix a medium mixture of turquoise with water and paint over the lines. Remember to paint inside the eyes and nose of the skull cherries.

8. Ink the outlines of your painting.

GHOULISH JELLY

SUPPLIES

Fine round brush
Medium round brush
Pen to outline

COLORS

   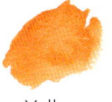 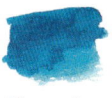

Emerald   Cadmium yellow hue   Alizarin crimson hue   Yellow ochre   Turquoise

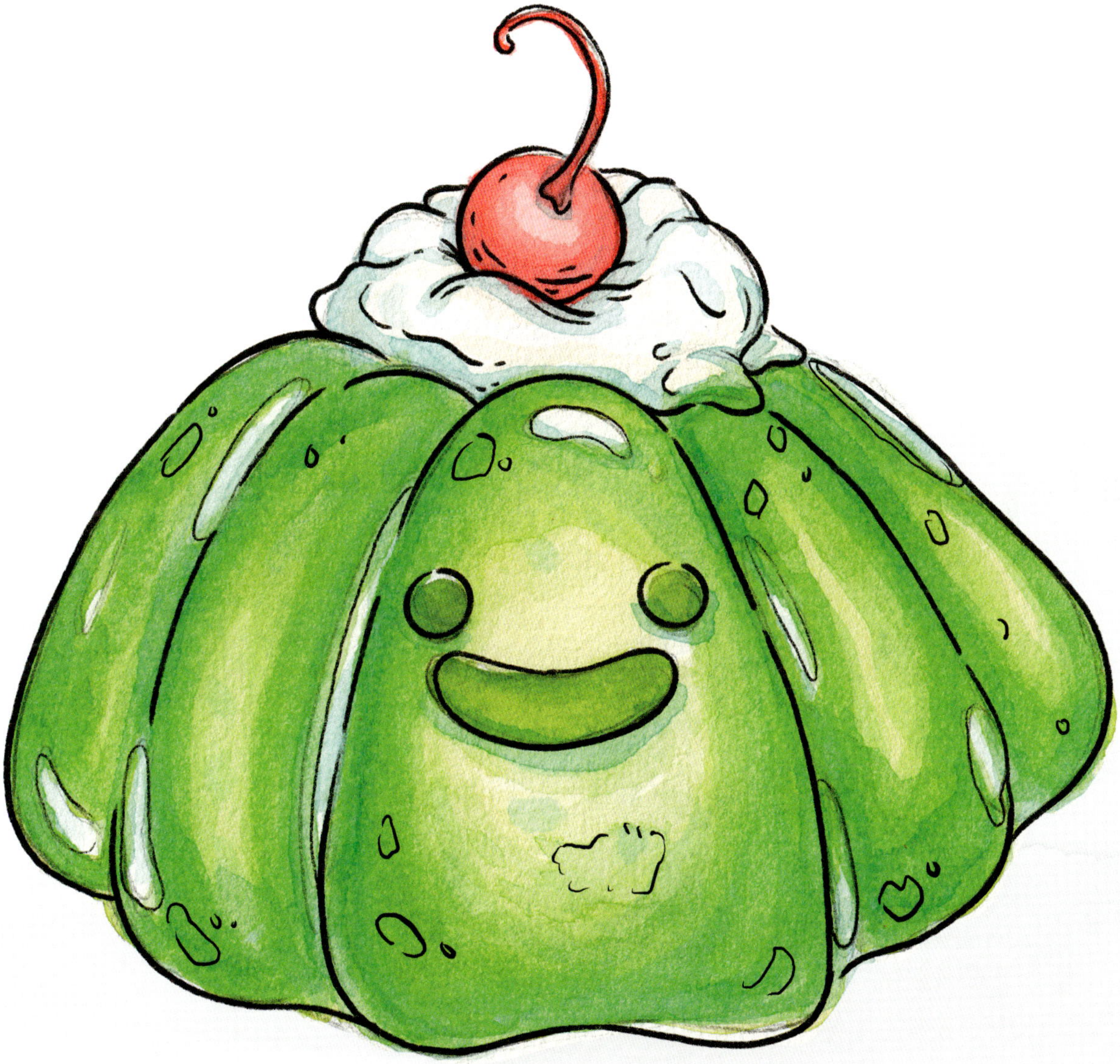

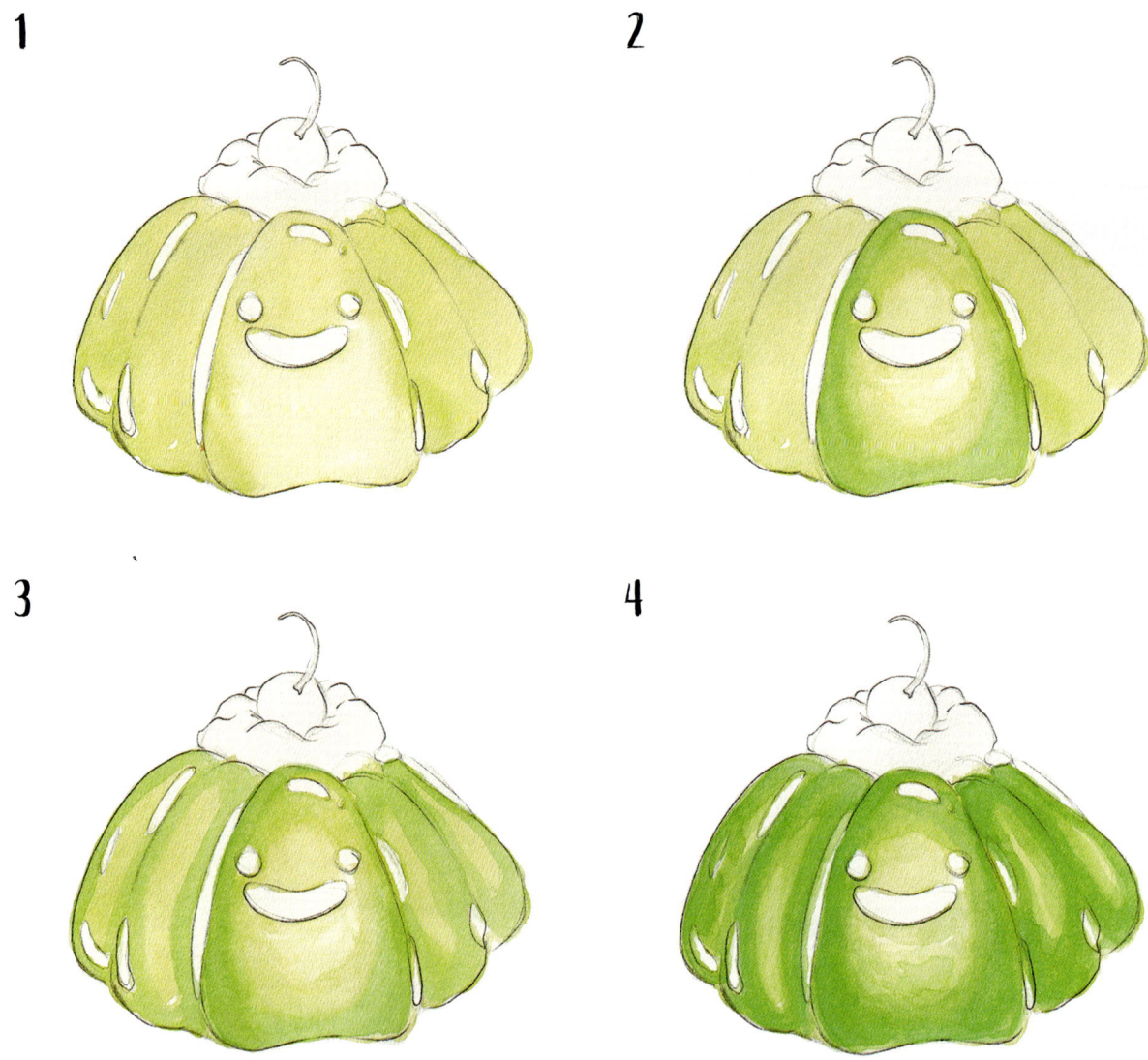

1. For this painting we'll use the white of the paper for the highlights in the finished painting. First lightly draw outlines of the areas to avoid painting. Using a mix of half emerald and half cadmium yellow hue, paint a wash over the jelly and let dry.

2. Using less water, paint the mixture on the middle section of the jelly, starting around the outline and painting inward. Let dry.

3. Repeat step 2 to paint the rest of the jelly sections. Remember to avoid the highlight outlines.

4. Using the same mixture, with even less water, continue to build up values in the jelly.

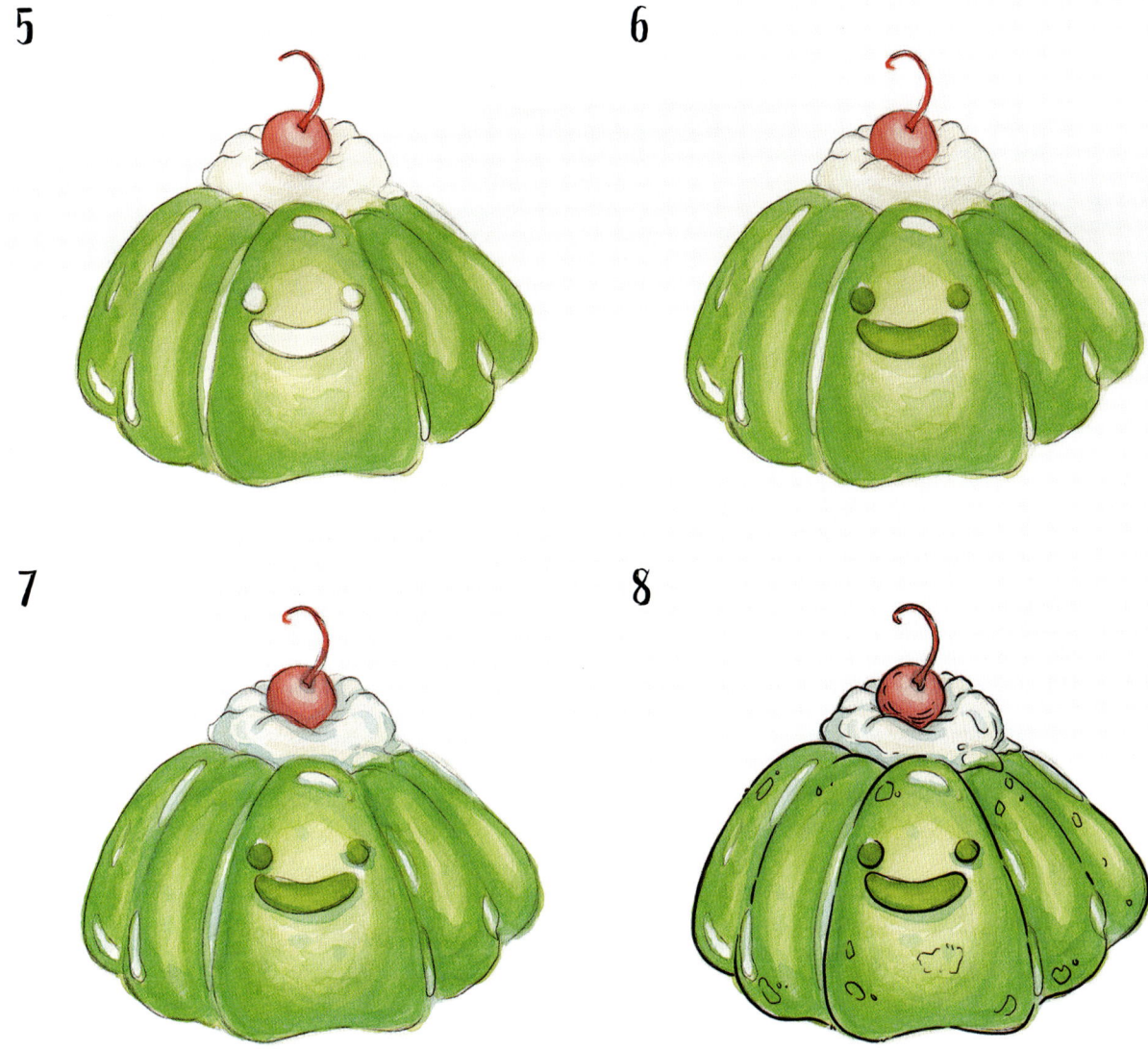

5. Use alizarin crimson hue to paint the cherry. Paint the body of the cherry with a wash and add thicker paint to the bottom of the cherry. Apply a thicker layer of paint to the stem of the cherry as well. Then add a very light wash of yellow ochre to the cream on top of the jelly.

6. Paint the inside of the face with a mixture of emerald and turquoise.

7. Using turquoise apply a light wash and paint along the outline of the image.

8. Ink the outline of the painting.

AHH!VOCADO TOAST

SUPPLIES

Fine round brush
Medium round brush
Pen to outline

COLORS

Yellow
ochre

Burnt
sienna

Burnt
umber

Cadmium
yellow hue

Emerald

Cadmium
orange hue

Prussian
blue

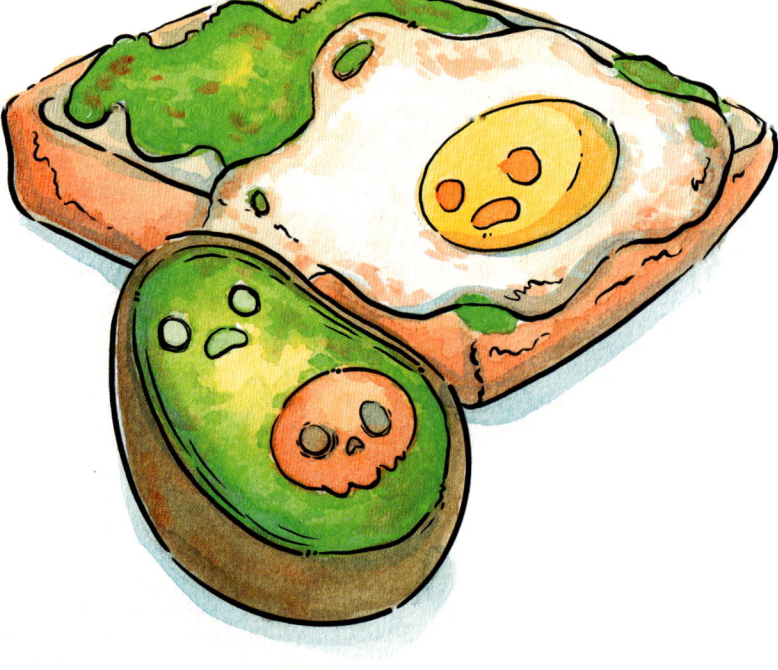

1

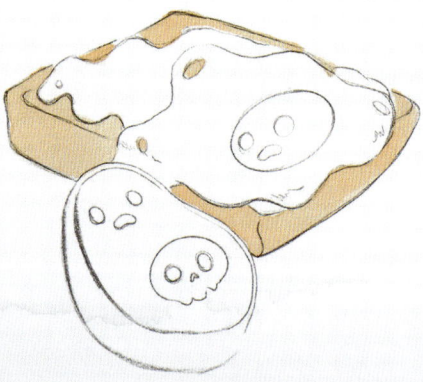

2

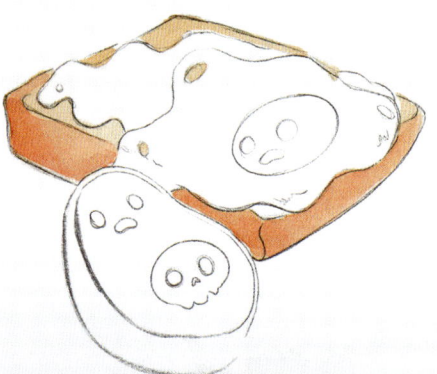

1. Paint a light wash of yellow ochre to the toast and let dry.

2. Paint another light wash of burnt sienna on the crust of the toast. Let partially dry before moving to step 3.

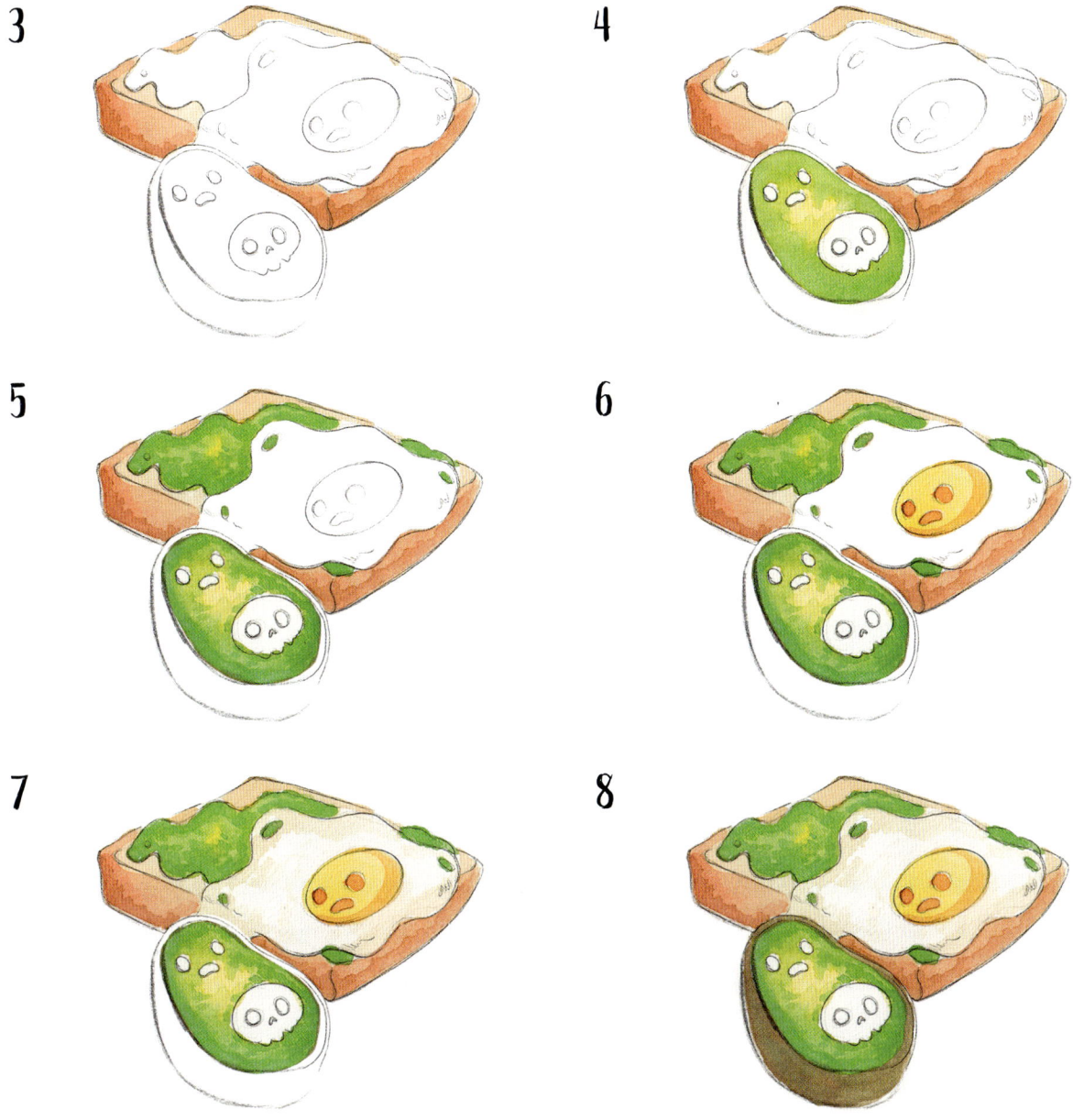

3. Use a light mix of burnt umber to paint the bottom of the toast, and let dry.

4. Paint a light wash of cadmium yellow hue on the avocado. While the paint is wet, mix cadmium yellow hue and emerald and paint around the outskirts of the avocado, painting inward and stopping before you reach the center. Let dry.

5. Use the same technique from step 4 to paint the guacamole.

6. Mix emerald and burnt sienna. Using more pigment and less water, paint the base of the avocado and let dry.

7. Paint the yolk with cadmium yellow hue and let dry. Then use cadmium orange hue to paint the face of the yolk, as well as an ellipse on the bottom of the yolk to give it some shading.

8. Using yellow ochre, paint a mixture of 80% water and 20% paint on the outline of the egg.

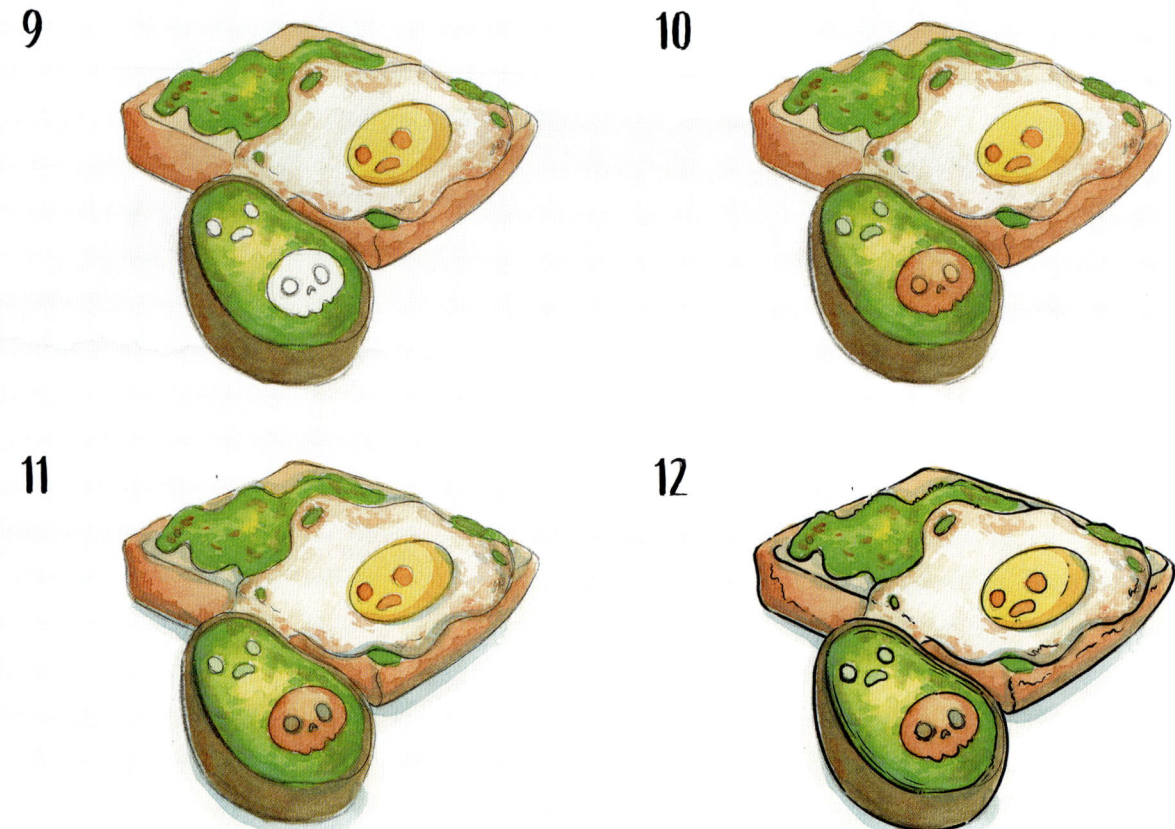

9. Use a light mixture of burnt sienna and add speckles or blots around the egg, as well as the avocado and guacamole.

10. Paint the face of the avocado with emerald.

11. For the avocado pit, paint first with yellow ochre and, while still wet, apply burnt sienna to the base of the skull and paint inward.

12. Use Prussian blue to paint shadows, as well as the eyes for the skull pit.

BOO-HOOTIFUL OWL

SUPPLIES

Fine round brush
Medium round brush
Pen to outline

COLORS

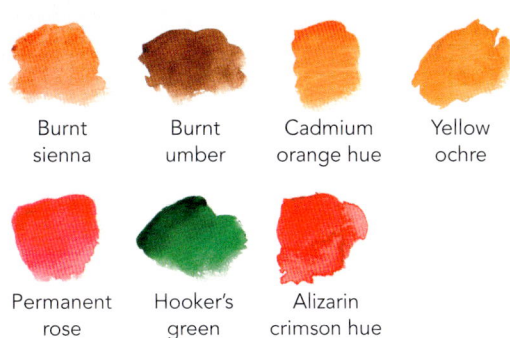

Burnt sienna

Burnt umber

Cadmium orange hue

Yellow ochre

Permanent rose

Hooker's green

Alizarin crimson hue

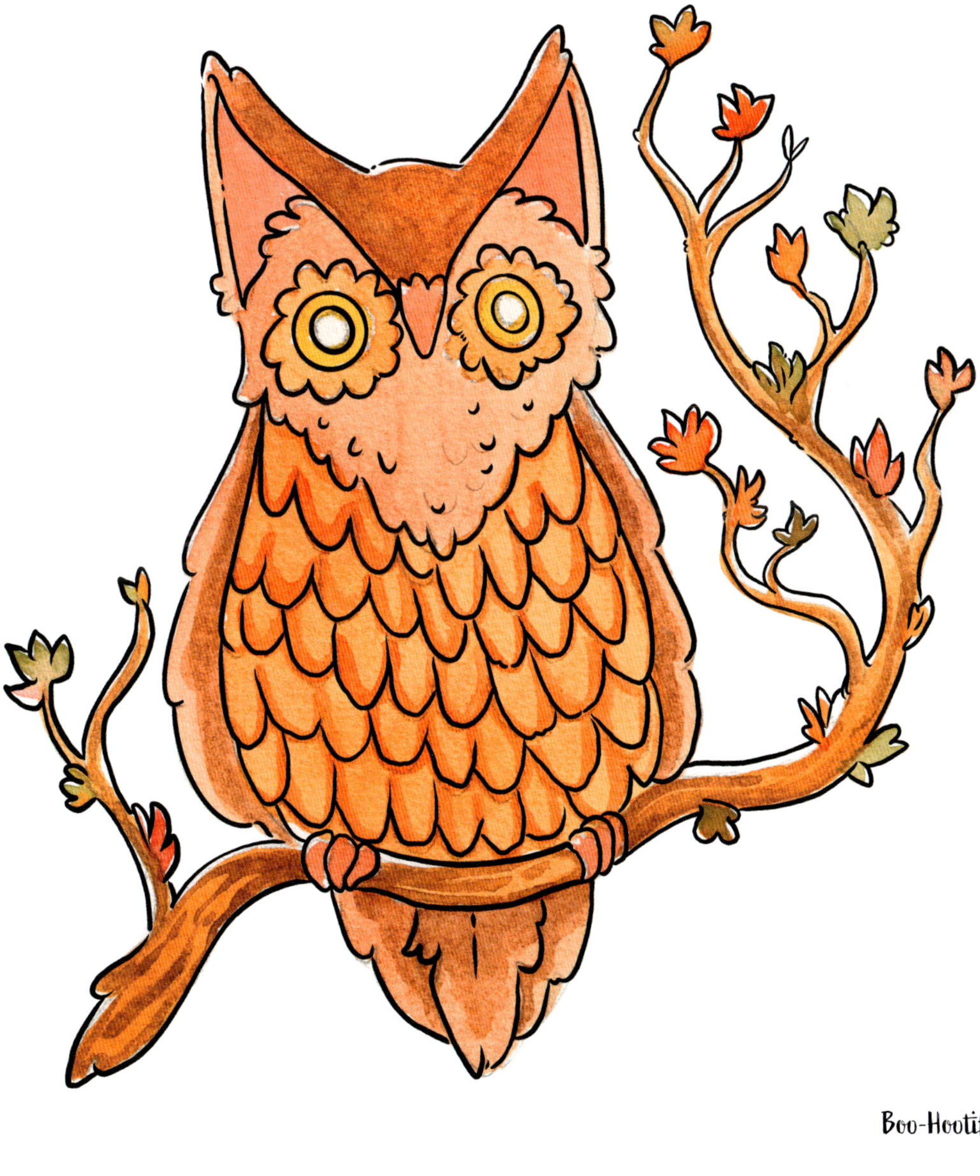

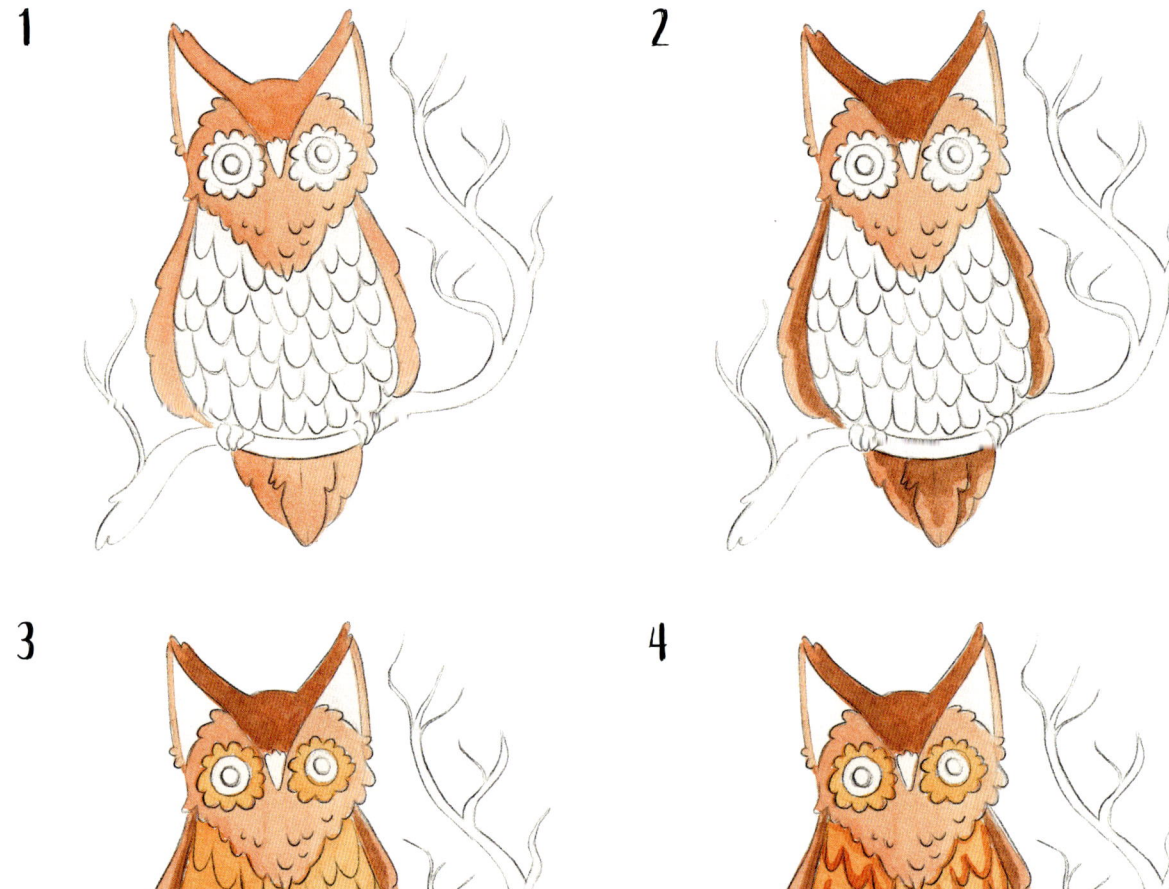

1. Using a small- to medium-size brush, paint the body of the owl (avoiding the belly) with burnt sienna. Let this layer of paint dry before moving to the next step.

2. Use a smaller brush to paint on burnt umber on parts of the previous layer:

   — Top of owl's head

   — Inside of owl's wings

   — Top of owl's tail feathers

3. For the belly and outer circle of the eyes, paint on cadmium orange hue and let dry.

4. Using a finer-tipped brush, use burnt sienna to paint the U-shaped bottoms of the feathers on the belly of the owl.

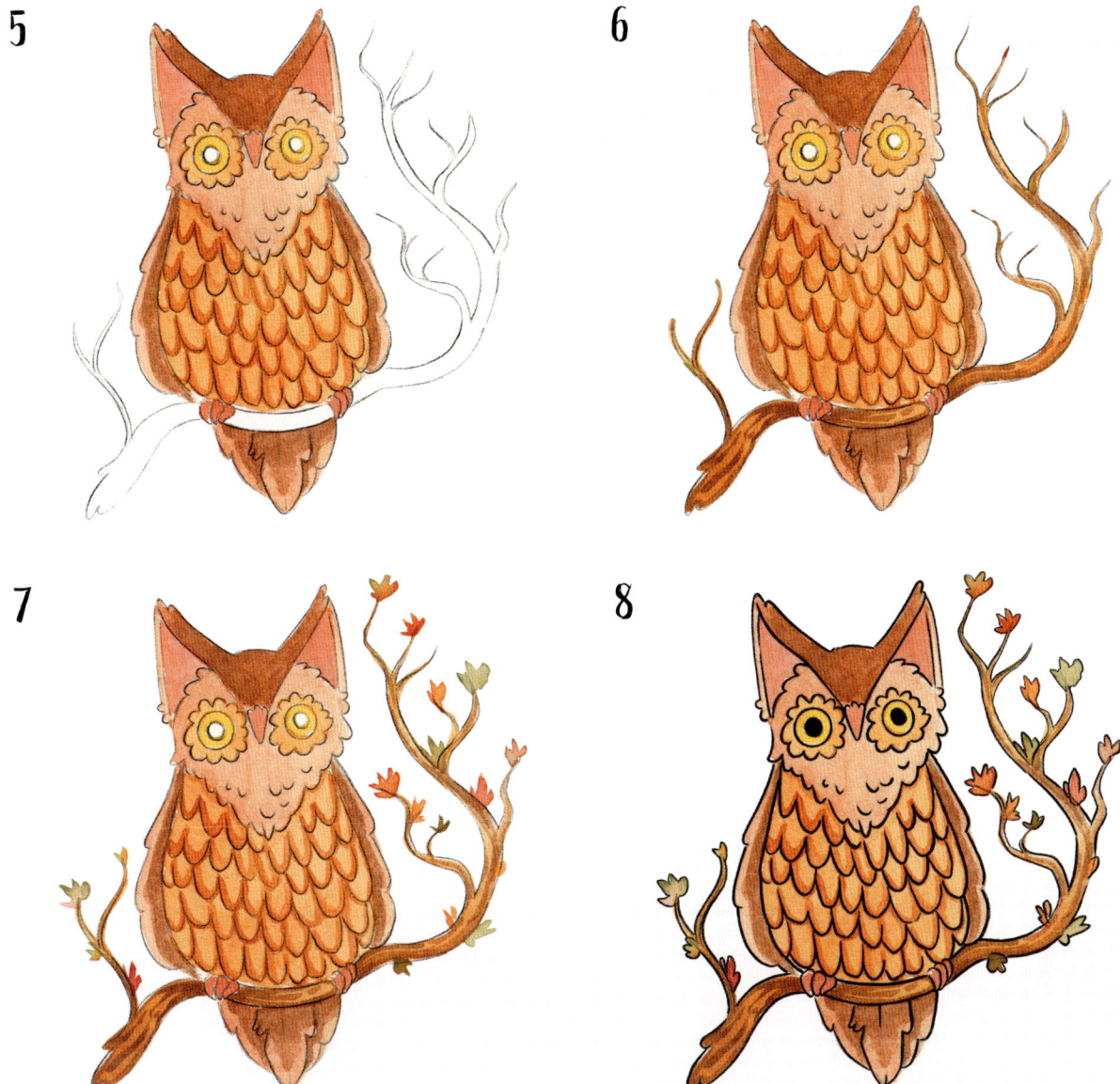

5. Mix a small amount of yellow ochre and permanent rose together and, using a fine-tip brush, paint the inside of the ears, the feet, and the beak. For this step I also used yellow ochre to paint the inner circle of the eyes.

6. Use cadmium orange hue, or any brown color, to paint the branch. Let dry. Then use burnt sienna to paint fine lines in the branch to add tree texture.

7. Select colors for your leaves. I chose Hooker's green, cadmium orange hue, and alizarin crimson hue to give it a fall-time feel. For the leaves, paint a tapering line by pressing lightly on the paper and then harder as you complete the brushstroke. You want the lines to start off thin and end thicker. Paint these lines a couple of times and connect them at the base.

8. Ink your painting.

BEWITCHING BAT

SUPPLIES

Fine round brush
Medium round brush
Pen to outline

COLORS

  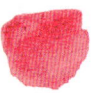  

Yellow ochre · Burnt umber · Purple lake · Permanent rose · Turquoise

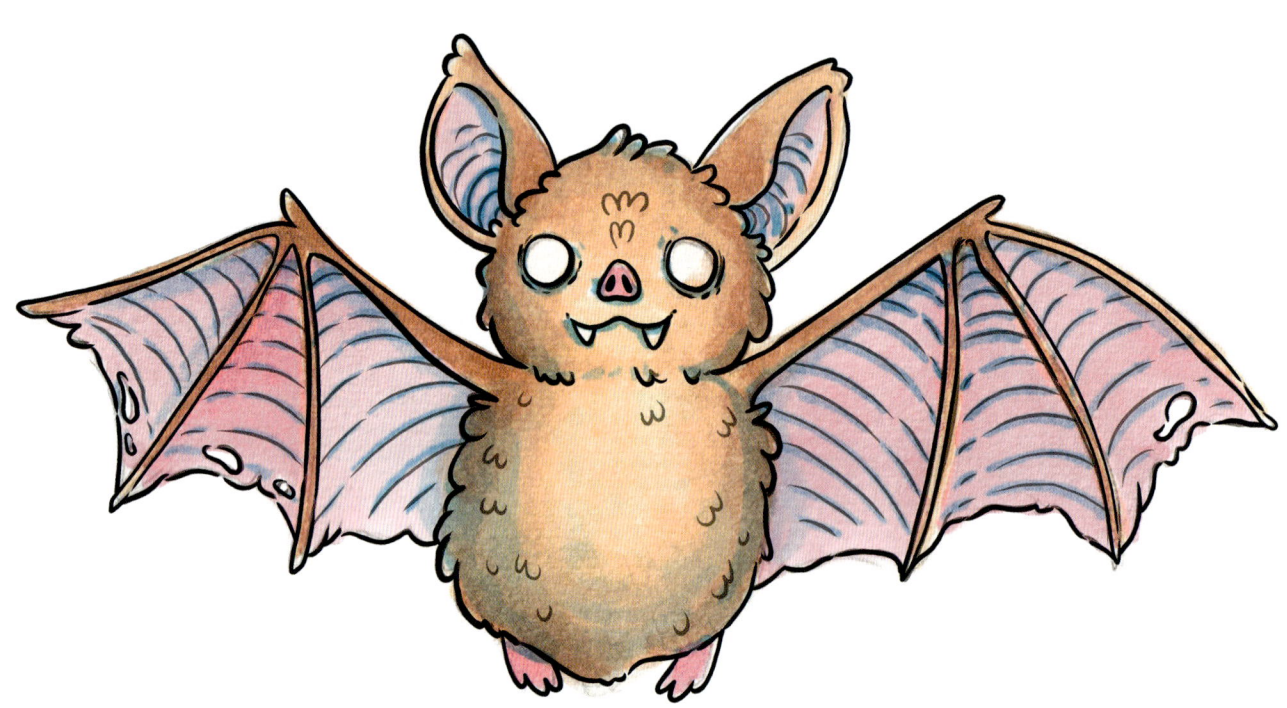

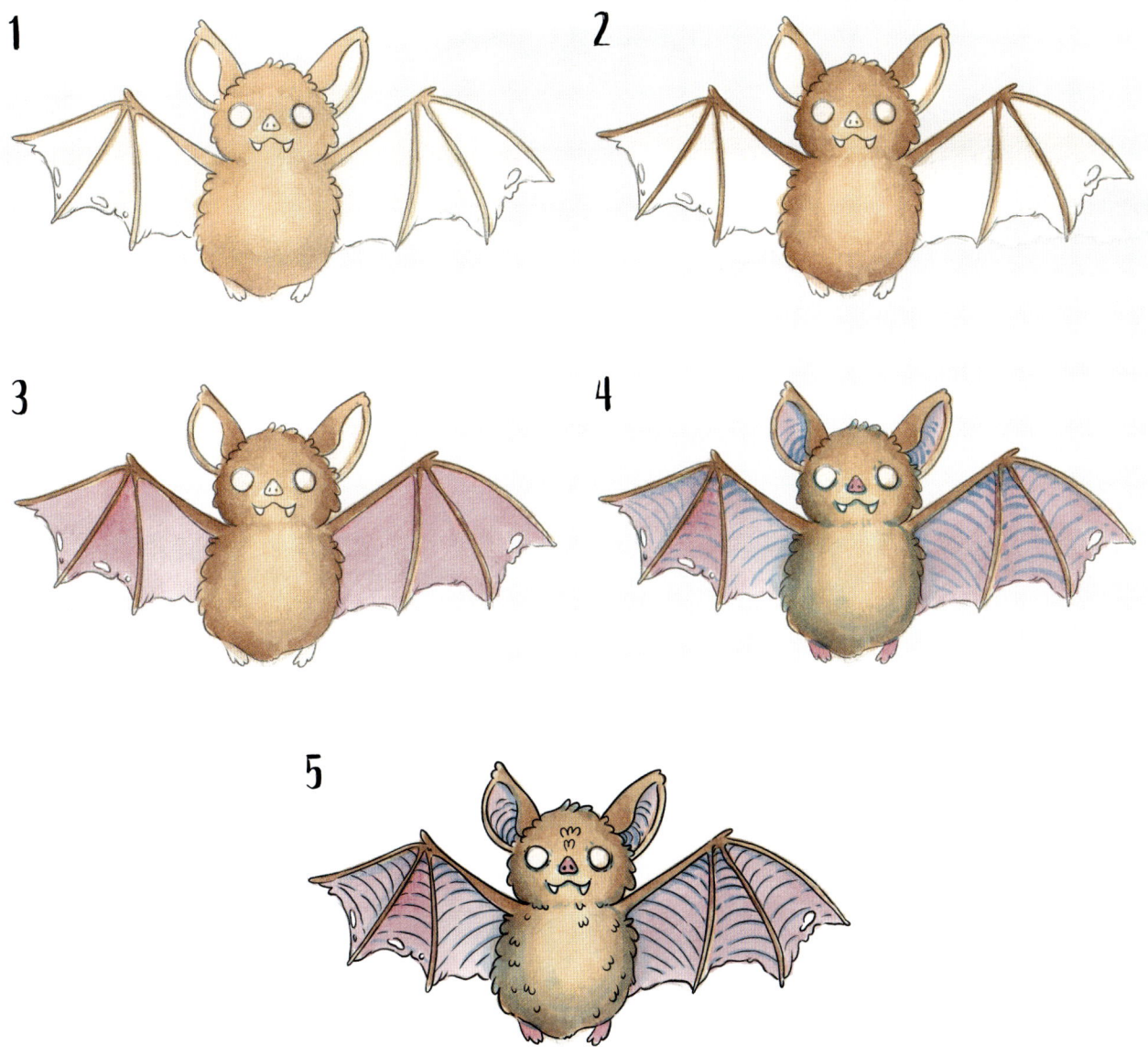

1. Apply a light wash of yellow ochre to the body of the bat. While still damp, apply burnt umber, starting toward the edge of the body, painting inward.

2. Paint on a light layer of burnt umber around the body, painting inward and creating a gradient effect, leaving some of the previous layer exposed.

3. For the wings, paint on a light layer of purple lake.

4. Paint the inner ears with purple lake. For the nose and the feet, use permanent rose. For shadows, use a light layer of turquoise. Paint the lines on the wings, as well as the ears, with turquoise.

5. Ink your painting.

FOXY FIEND

SUPPLIES

Fine round brush
Medium round brush
Pen to outline

COLORS

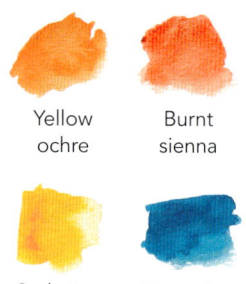

Yellow ochre

Burnt sienna

Cadmium yellow hue

Turquoise

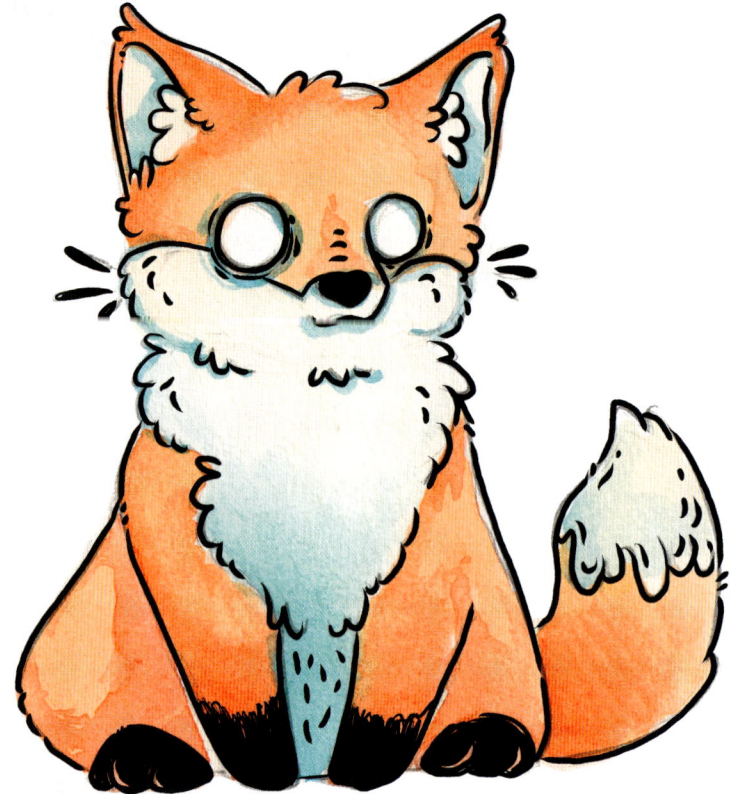

1. Using yellow ochre and a medium-size brush, apply a very light wash to the body of the fox. Avoid painting the eyes and let dry.

2. Mix together 50% burnt sienna with 50% cadmium yellow hue. Apply a medium wash to the legs, body, top of face, and lower half of the tail. Let dry.

3. Using burnt sienna and a medium-size brush, paint a darker layer on top of the previous layer. For the head, paint a gradient, starting from the top of the ears and working down. Paint a small amount above the nose, painting upward.

For the front legs, start at the bottom and paint upward. For the back legs, start painting right above the feet and paint upward. For the tail, start at the base and paint upward.

4. Use a light wash of turquoise for the shadows on the stomach. Start at the bottom and paint upward, making a gradient effect. Do the same in the white of the tail, as well as the ears. Paint around the eyes and along the fur texture lines.

5. Ink your painting and shade in the black feet.

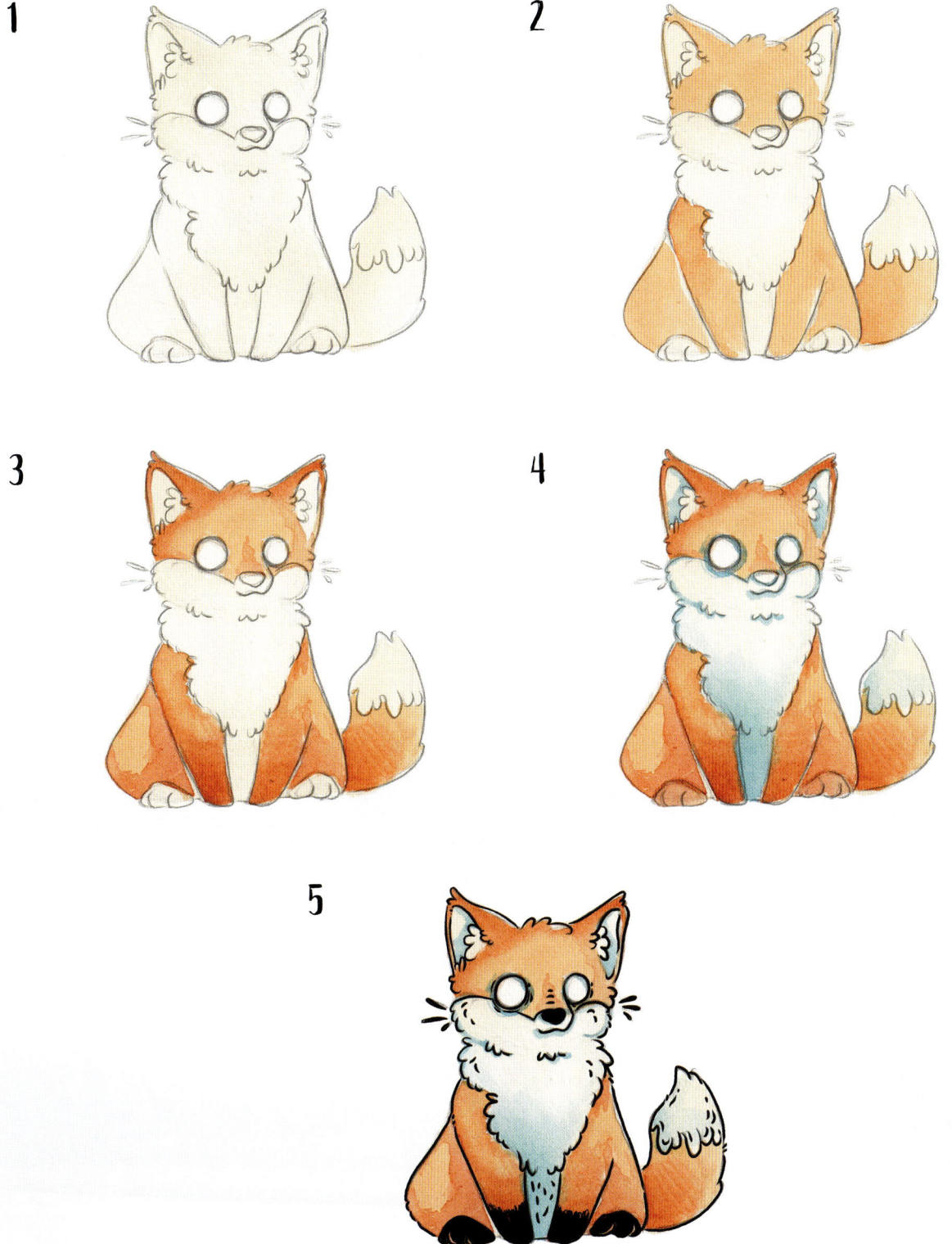

HEDGEHAG

SUPPLIES

Fine round brush
Medium round brush
Pen to outline
White pen for highlights

COLORS

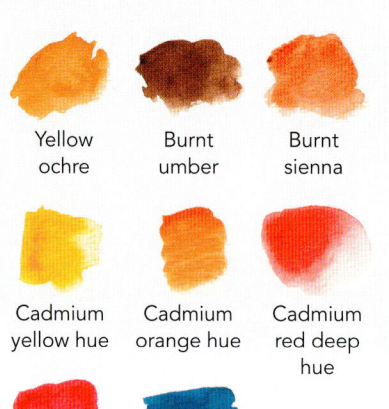

Yellow ochre

Burnt umber

Burnt sienna

Cadmium yellow hue

Cadmium orange hue

Cadmium red deep hue

Permanent rose

Turquoise

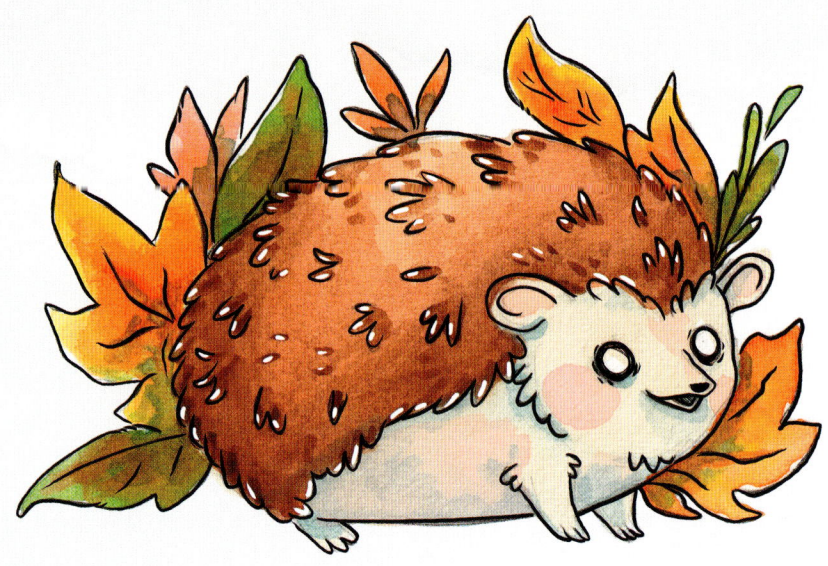

1. Paint the body of the hedgehog with a light wash of yellow ochre and let dry.

2. With a mix of 50% burnt umber and 50% burnt sienna, paint a light wash on the back of the hedgehog. Paint a darker layer on the back of the hedgehog, starting from the bottom and painting upward to create a gradient technique. Paint a medium wash of burnt umber on the bottom of the hedgehog's back.

3. Use a smaller-tipped brush to paint burnt umber on the quills. Choose natural leaf colors and start by painting each leaf with one color. Then use the wet-on-wet technique with a different color, letting the colors bleed into each other. For example, I painted one of the leaves cadmium yellow hue and then painted cadmium orange hue and cadmium red deep hue on top.

4. Paint on a very light wash of permanent rose on the underside of the belly, as well as the cheeks, inner ears, and above the nose. For shading, paint on a light wash of turquoise on the bottom of the body.

5. Ink in your painting

6. Use a white pin and ink the tips of the quills.

1

2

3

4

5

6

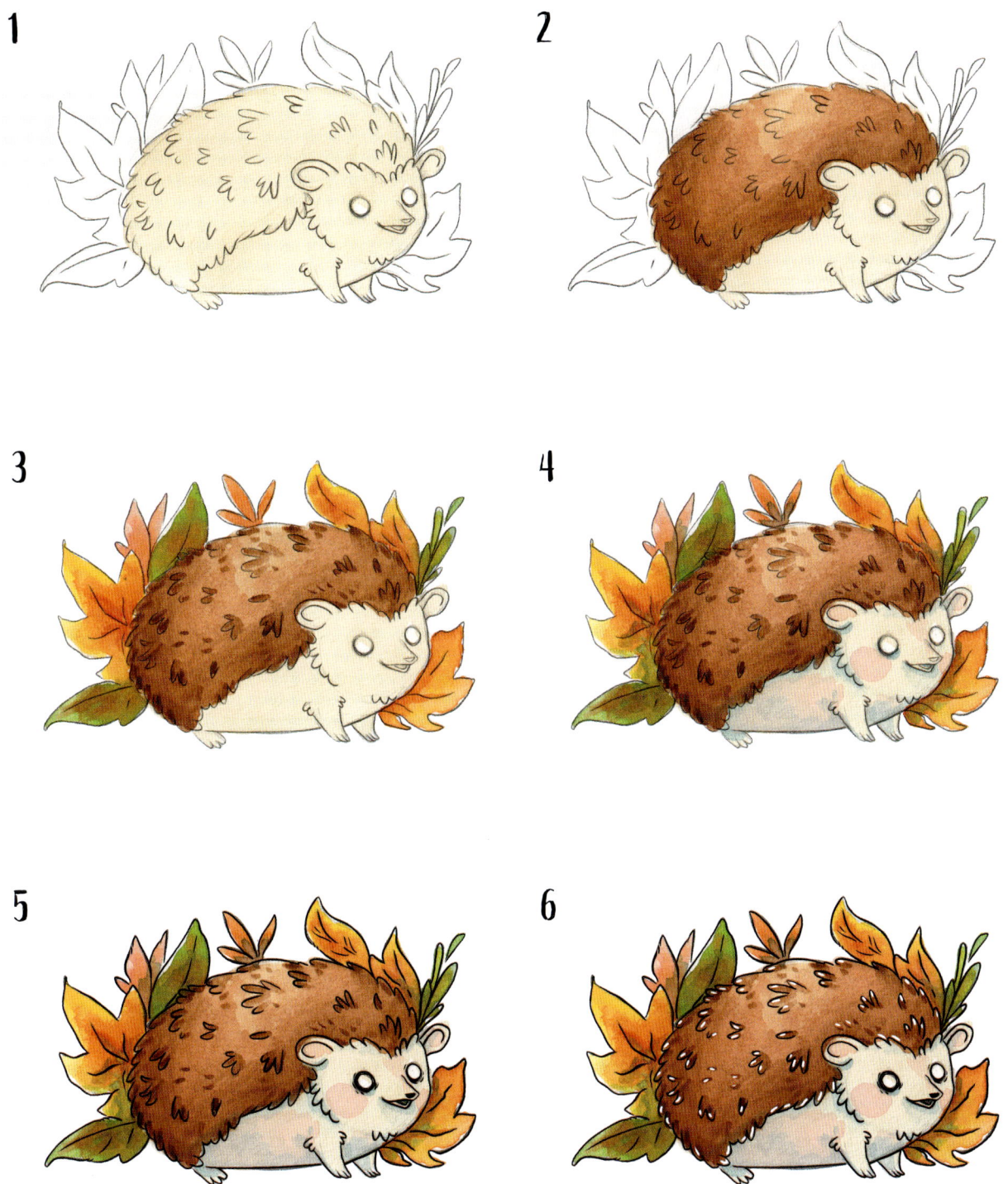

HAUNTED TEAPOT

SUPPLIES

Fine round brush
Medium round brush
Pen to outline

COLORS

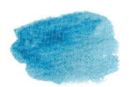

Hooker's green Cerulean blue hue

Cadmium yellow hue Burnt sienna

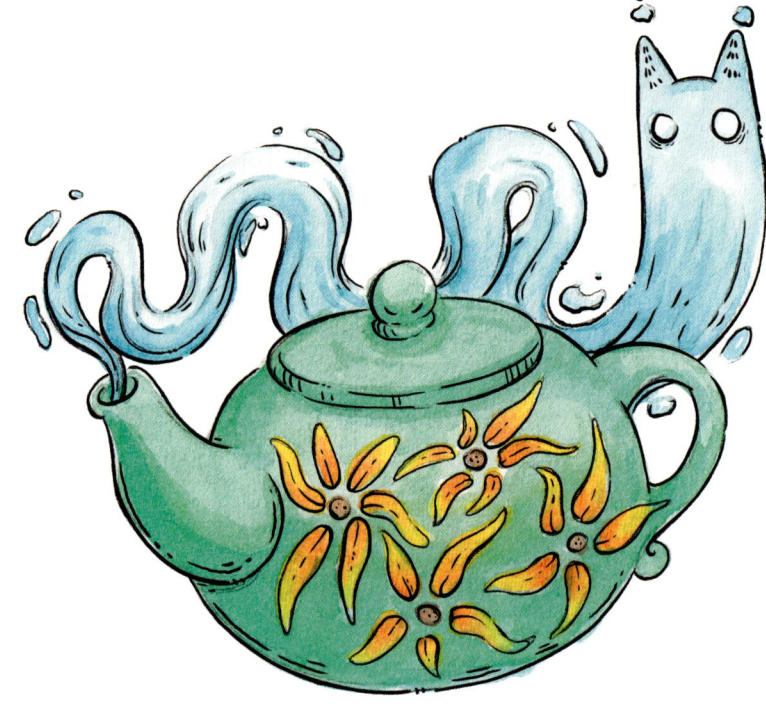

1. Mix together equal parts Hooker's green with cerulean blue hue and apply a medium wash on the teapot, avoiding the flowers. Let dry.

2. Apply a darker layer of the mixture from step 1 for shading. Paint the bottom area of the teapot and the outline of the lid.

3. Paint the petals of the flowers with cadmium yellow hue. While still damp, add a light mixture of burnt sienna to the base of the flowers and let it bleed into the yellow. Paint the middle of the flower with burnt sienna.

4. Wet the ghost and use the wet-on-wet technique to paint cerulean blue hue along the outline of the ghost, letting it bleed into the center. Let dry.

5. With a darker mixture of cerulean blue hue, use a fine-tip brush to paint the details within the body of the ghost. I also used cerulean blue hue to paint shading on the bottom body of the ghost.

6. Ink in your haunted teapot.

1

2

3

4

5

6

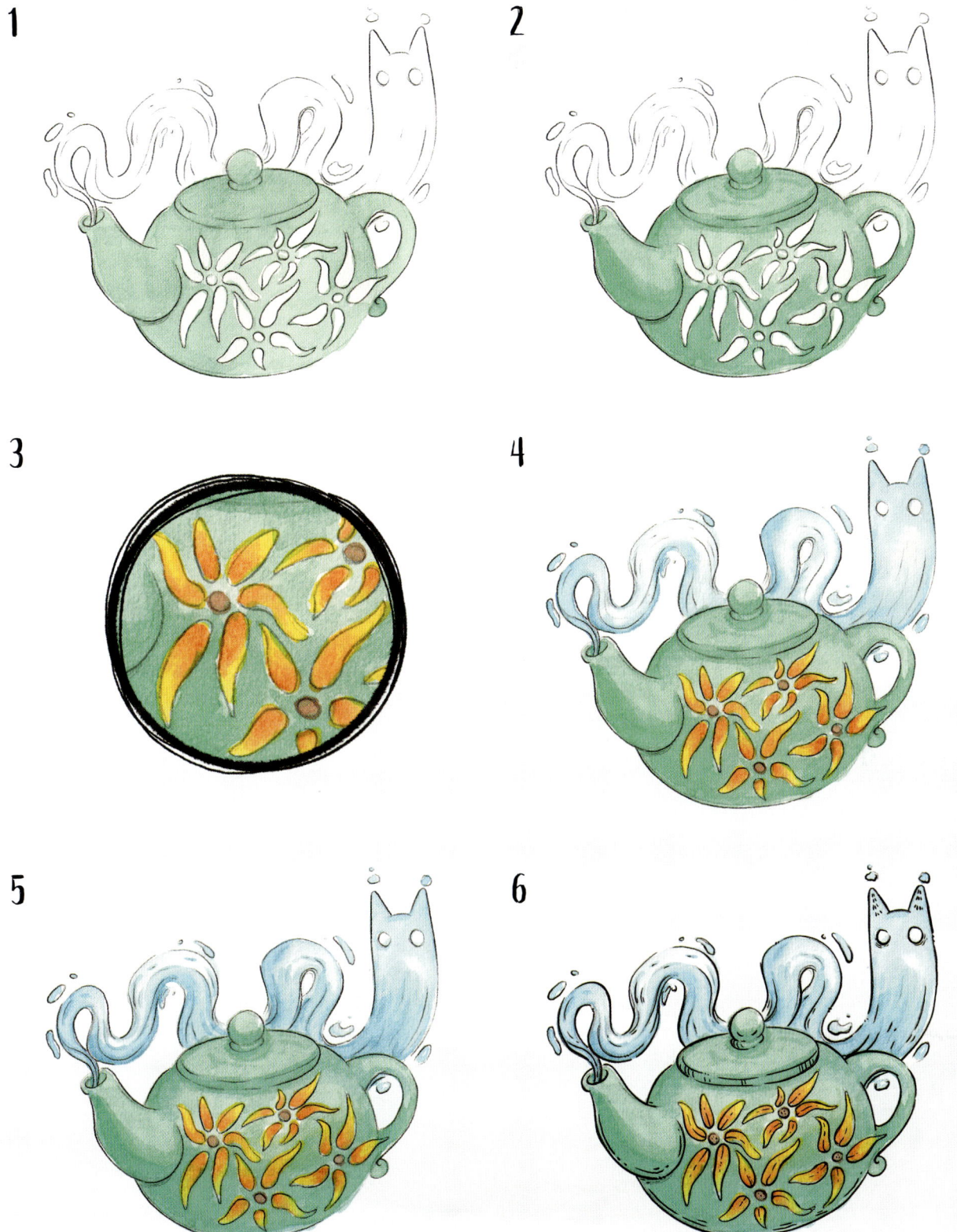

SPIRITED CANDLE

SUPPLIES

Fine round brush
Medium round brush
Pen to outline

COLORS

Cadmium   Yellow ochre
yellow hue

Turquoise   Cadmium
orange hue

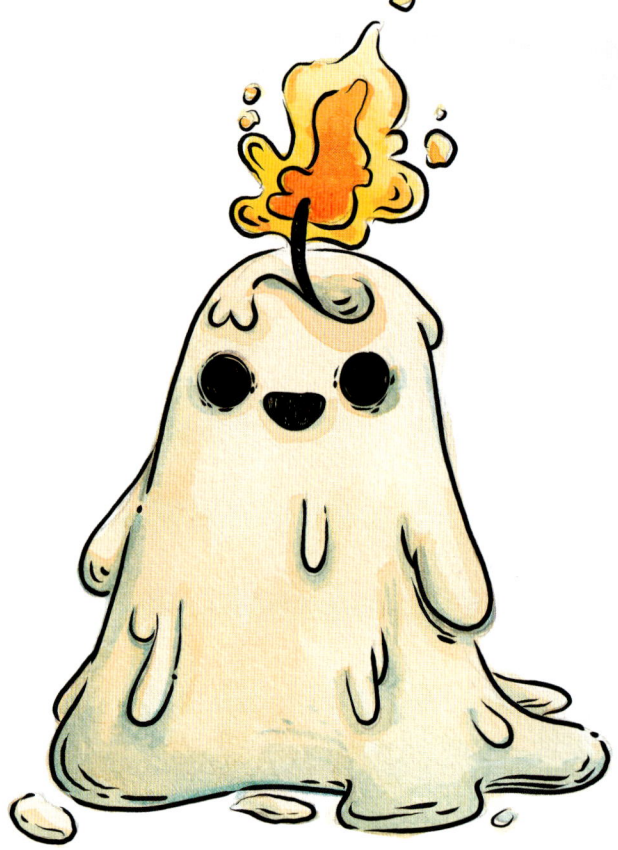

1. Mix equal parts cadmium yellow hue and yellow ochre. You only need a small amount of paint mixed with a lot of water to paint the body of the ghost candle.

2. Using the same mixture from step 1, use less water and add some shading on the candle. Keep some of the previous painted layer exposed to add highlighting.

3. Using a fine-tipped brush with turquoise, paint along the bottom of the lines to add shadows. Apply a light wash of turquoise to the bottom of the ghost candle.

4. For the candle flame, paint on a medium wash of cadmium yellow hue. Starting from the bottom of the candle, paint upward and let dry.

5. Paint the inner part of the flame using cadmium orange hue. You can also add a few brushstrokes of orange on the bottom of the flame.

6. Ink the outline of your painting. Fill in the eyes and mouth.

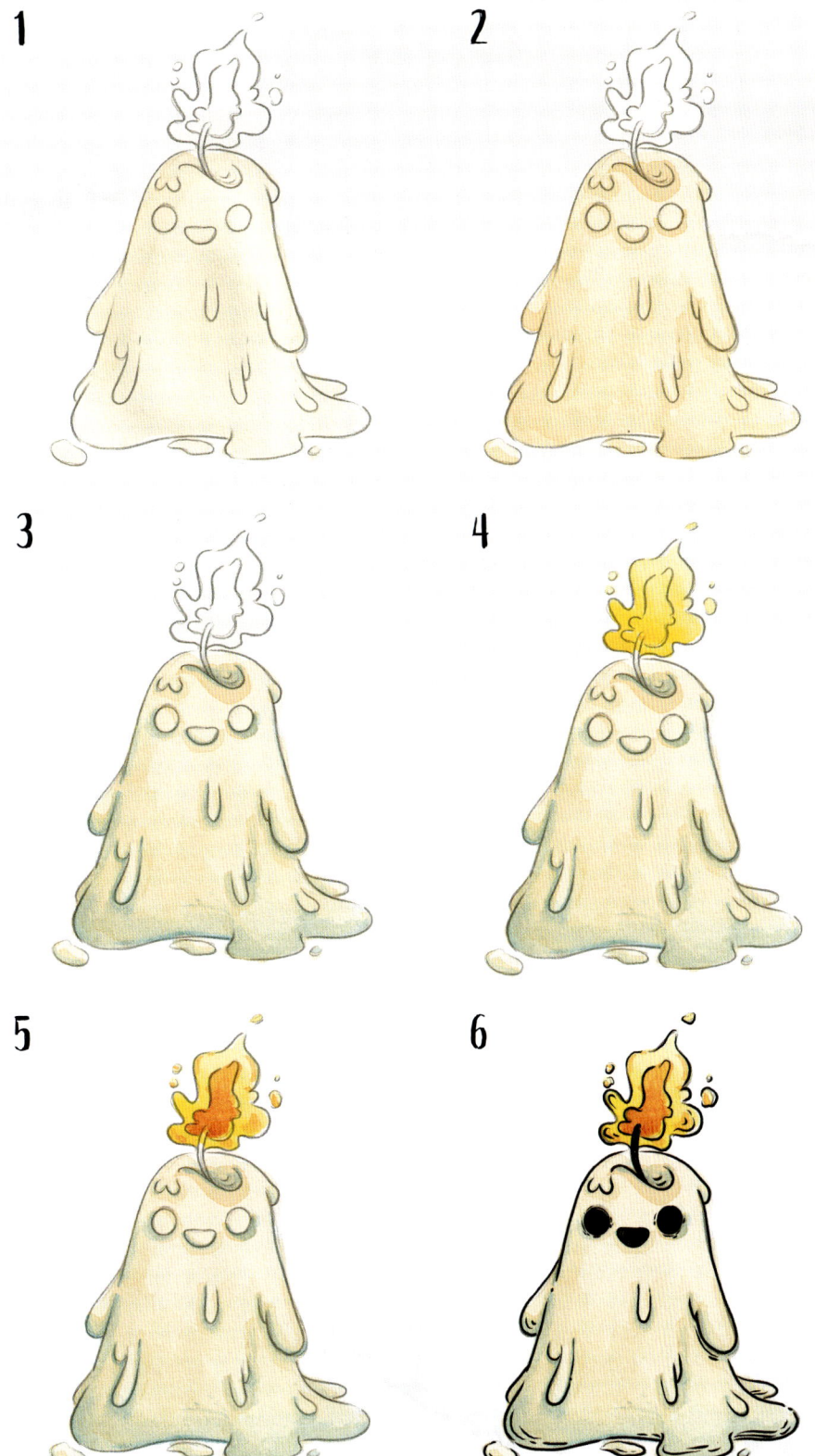

1

2

3

4

5

6

BOO TUNE PLAYER

SUPPLIES

Fine round brush
Medium round brush
Pen to outline
White pen for highlights

COLORS

  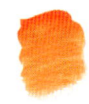

Emerald   Permanent   Cadmium
              rose   orange hue

Dioxazine   Turquoise
purple

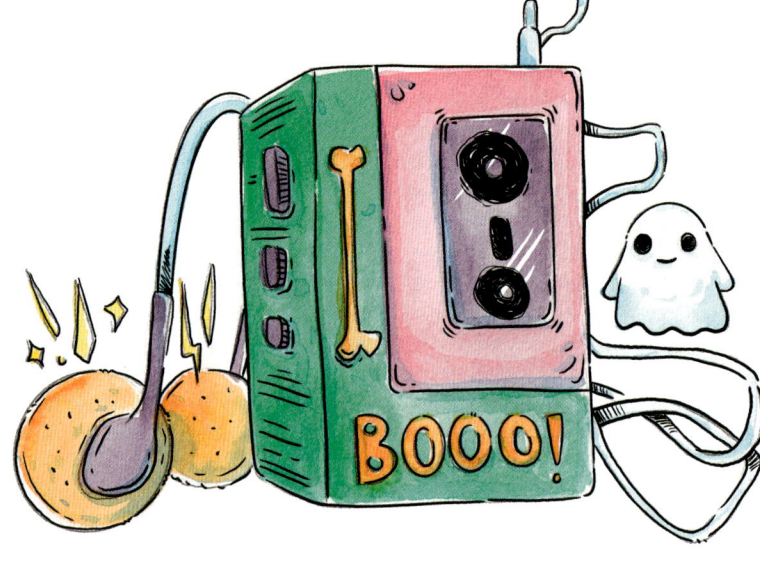

1. Using a medium brush, paint a medium wash of emerald on the left side of the cassette player. Add another thicker layer on the farthest left side to add shading.

2. On the upper right side of the player, paint a light wash of permanent rose. Add a thicker layer of permanent rose around the upper right section.

3. Using a fine round brush, use a medium mixture of cadmium orange hue to paint the bone and "Booo!," as well as the soft part of the headphones.

4. Paint a light layer of dioxazine purple on part of the headset, the side buttons, and the window of the player. Let dry.

5. Using turquoise, paint a light wash on the metal part of the headphones. Paint the wire for the headphones, but be sure to leave some white exposed (try painting the bottom section of the wire only.) Paint the bottom of the ghosts, as well as the bottom of the soft part of the headset. For shading on the cassette player paint along the lines.

6. Ink in your painting. To add reflection to the window of the player, use a white pin to add some highlights.

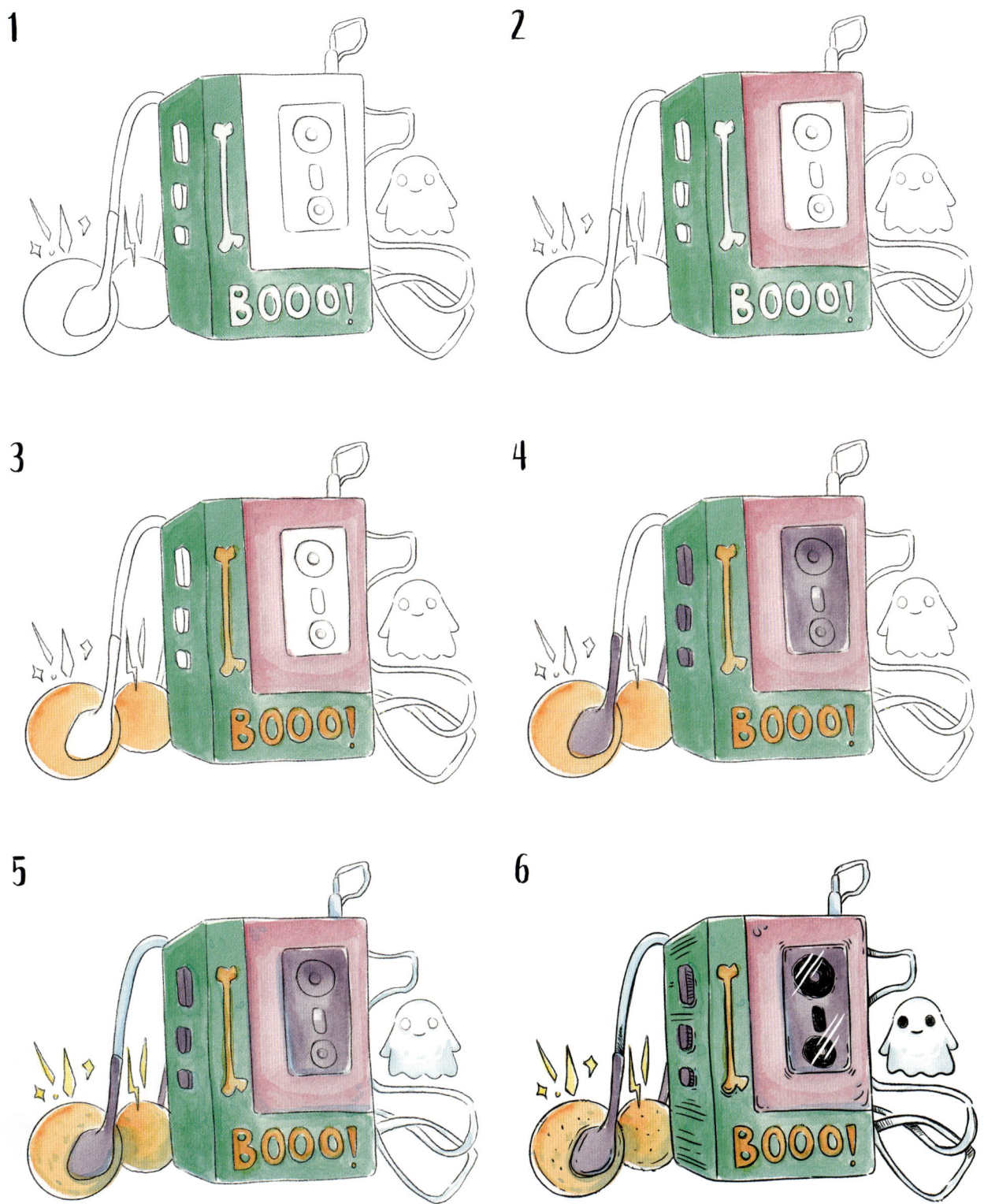

ECTOPLASMA TV

SUPPLIES

Fine round brush
Medium round brush
Pen to outline

COLORS

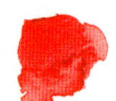

Burnt sienna   Cerulean blue hue   Alizarin crimson hue

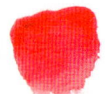
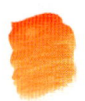

Cadmium yellow hue   Permanent rose

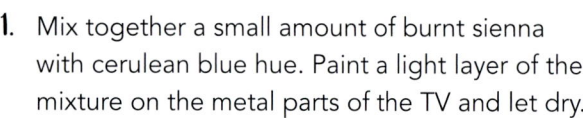

Purple lake   Cadmium orange hue

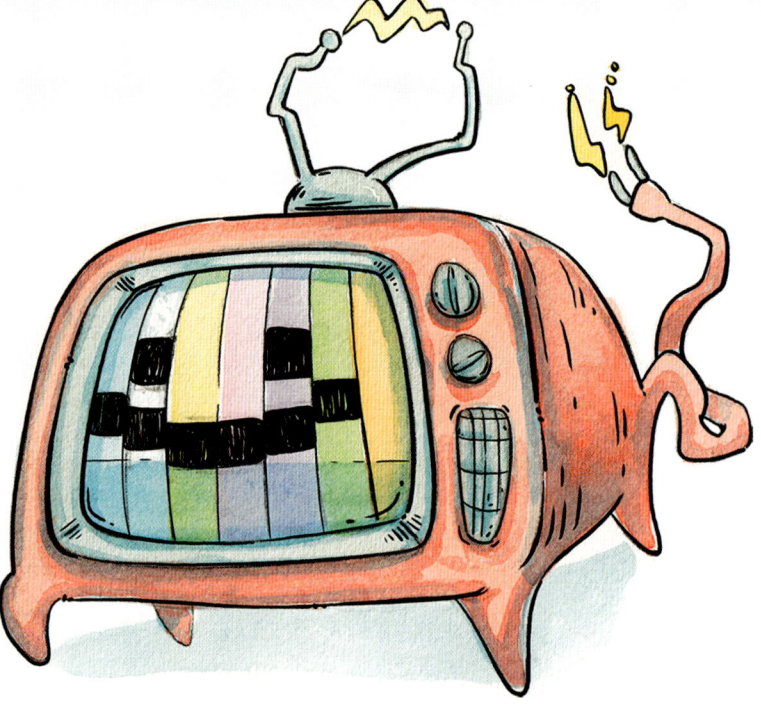

1. Mix together a small amount of burnt sienna with cerulean blue hue. Paint a light layer of the mixture on the metal parts of the TV and let dry.

2. Mix together 60% burnt sienna and 40% alizarin crimson hue and use a medium-size brush to paint a light wash on the TV. Let dry.

3. Paint a darker layer of the mixture from step 2 on the TV, leaving some of the previous painted layer exposed to give it a highlight effect. Let dry.

4. For this step mix a light mixture of cerulean blue hue, cadmium yellow hue, permanent rose, purple lake, and cadmium orange hue, and paint the stripes on the TV. Leave one of them blank (white). Let dry in between each strip you paint to avoid the colors bleeding into one another.

5. Using cerulean blue hue, paint a light wash on the bottom of the TV screen. Use the cerulean blue to paint a shadow underneath the TV. You can also add shading on the TV. Use cadmium yellow hue with a fine-tipped brush to paint in the electric bolts.

6. Ink your painting. Add some lines to the side of the TV for shading and fill in the blocks on the TV screen for the face.

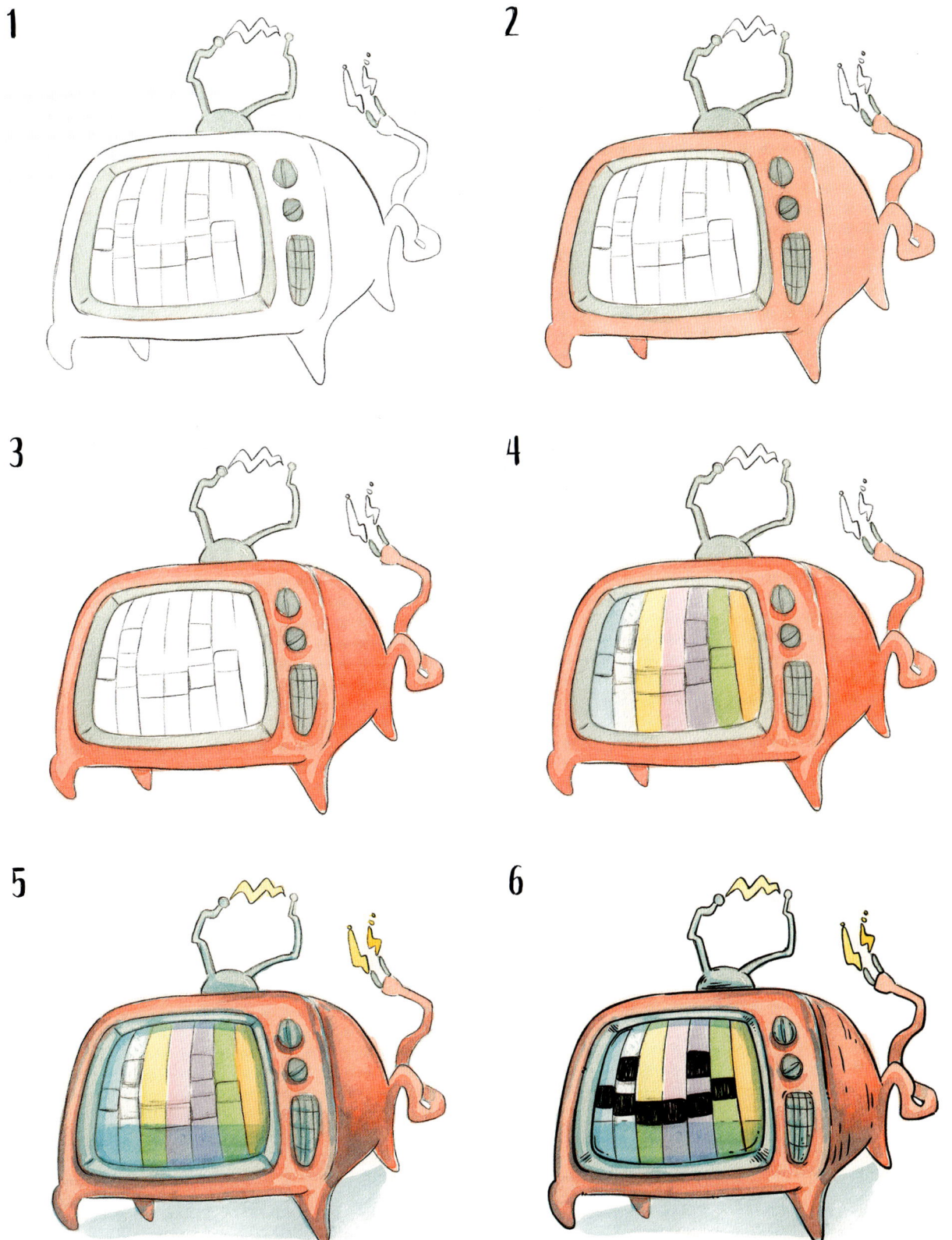

BUTTON SPIDERS

SUPPLIES

Fine round brush
Pen to outline

COLORS

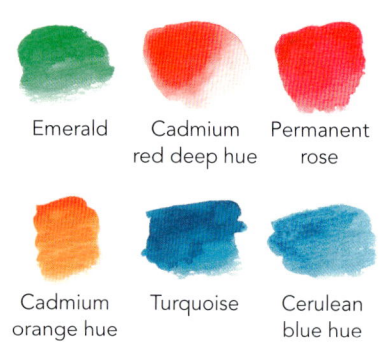

Emerald   Cadmium   Permanent
           red deep hue   rose

Cadmium   Turquoise   Cerulean
orange hue   blue hue

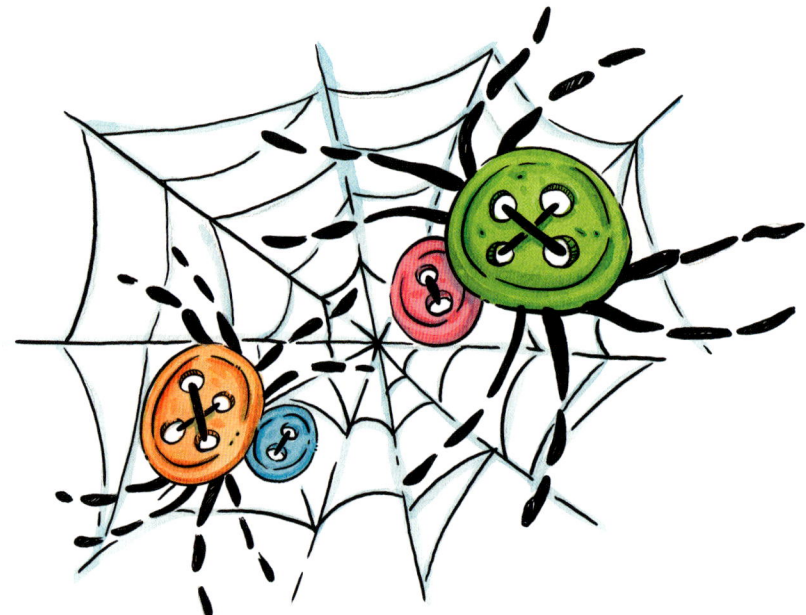

1. Using a fine round brush, add a wash of emerald to the larger button on the right spider. Let dry. Add shadows with a more concentrated emerald around the inside edges of the button.

2. With a clean brush, add a wash of cadmium red deep hue to the smaller button on the right spider. Let dry. Add shadows to this button with permanent rose.

3. Focusing on the left spider, paint a wash of cadmium orange hue on the larger button. Let dry. Add shadows to the button with the same color.

4. Use a wash of turquoise to paint the smaller button of the left spider. Let dry and add shadow lines with the same turquoise color.

5. Mix water and cerulean blue hue to make a very light blue shade. With a fine round brush, paint this light blue along the lines of the web.

6. Outline the drawing with pen. Fill the legs and the thread.

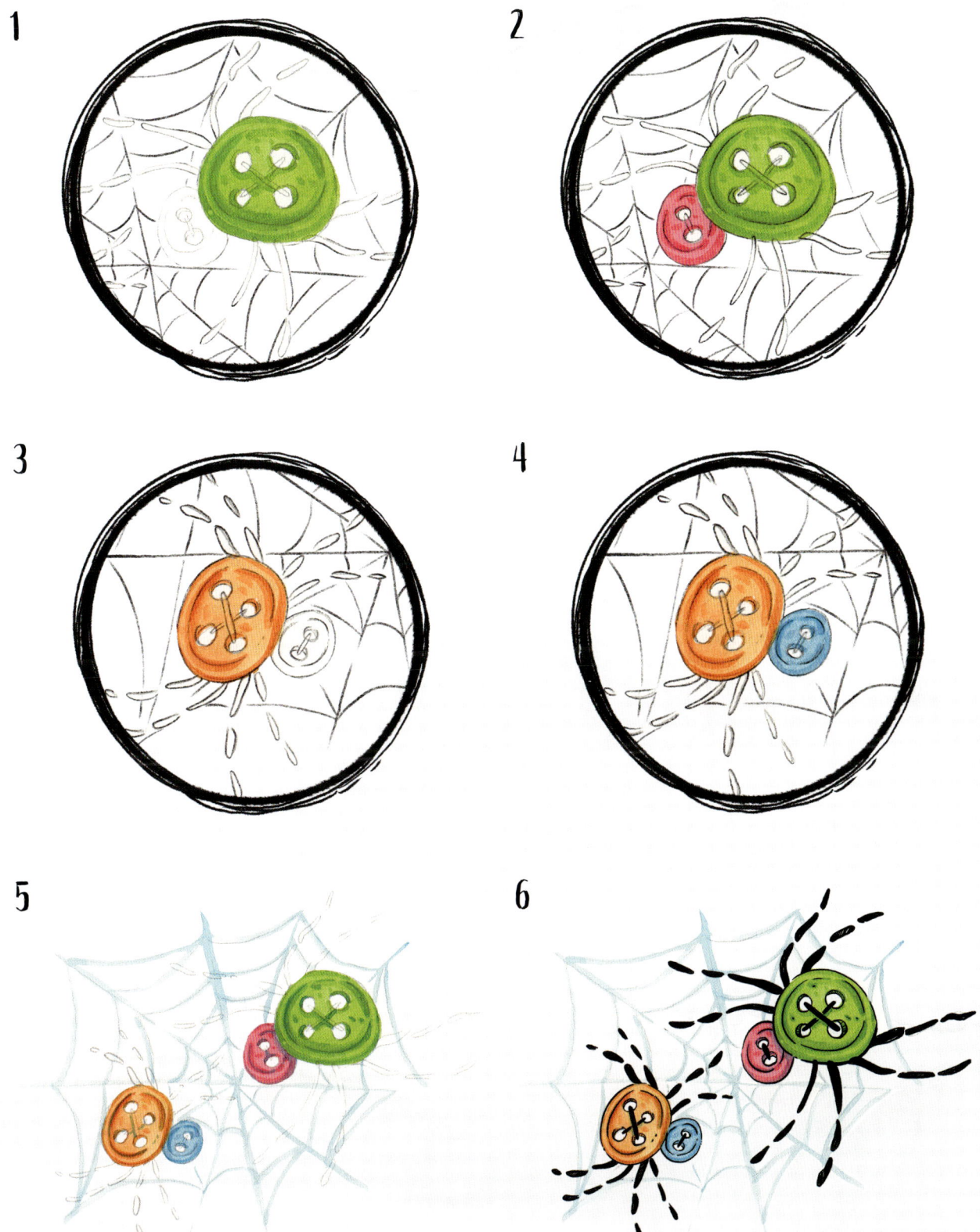

1

2

3

4

5

6

MACABRE MOTH

SUPPLIES

Fine round brush
Medium round brush
Pen to outline

COLORS

 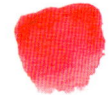 

Cadmium yellow hue   Permanent rose   Turquoise

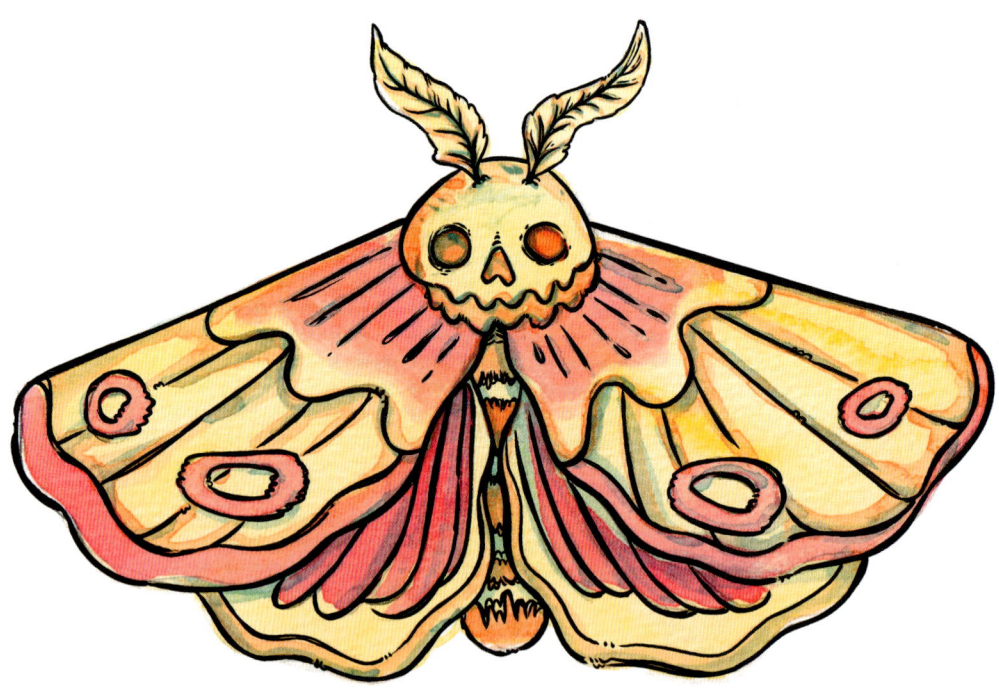

1. Use a medium brush to apply a medium wash of cadmium yellow hue on the body of the moth. Let dry.

2. On the top part of the wing, start by painting a gradient wash of permanent rose. In the middle part of the wing paint a medium wash of permanent rose inside the circle patterns, as well as the bottom of the middle section wing. On the bottom section of the wings, paint on a thicker layer of permanent rose inside the sectional area.

3. Mix a lot of water with a small amount of permanent rose and paint on with a smaller brush, such as size 4. Paint the lines on the antennae and the outskirts of the skull, including inside the eyes and nose. For the middle section use the brush to paint small lines and create stripes. Paint along the lines of the wings.

4. Use a light mixture of turquoise for shading. Paint along the lines of the moth, as well as the middle section of the body.

5. Ink the outlines of the moth.

1

2

3

4

5

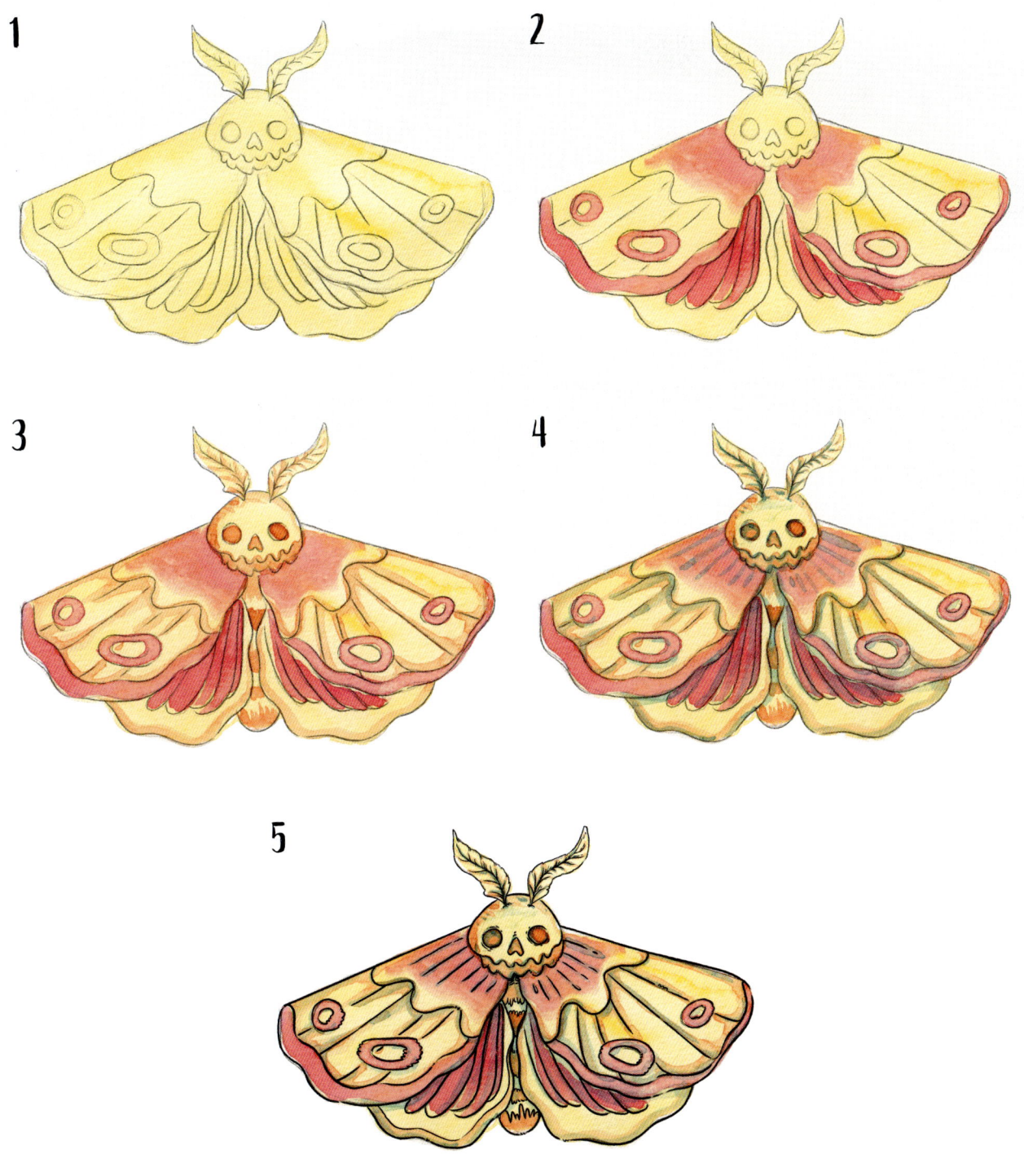

EXTRAS

I had so much fun designing the creepy cute paintings in this book that I created way more than we could fit in these pages! As an extra bonus, I am sharing those extra designs here. Scan the QR code provided to download the printable sketches. Print those out on your favorite watercolor paper and have fun painting.

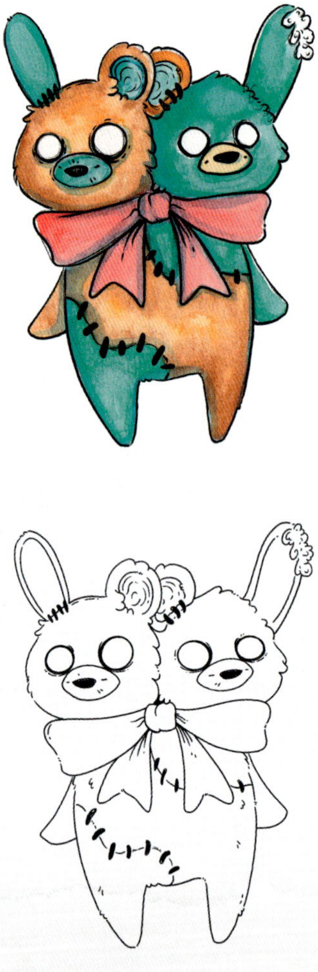

Bunny Bear

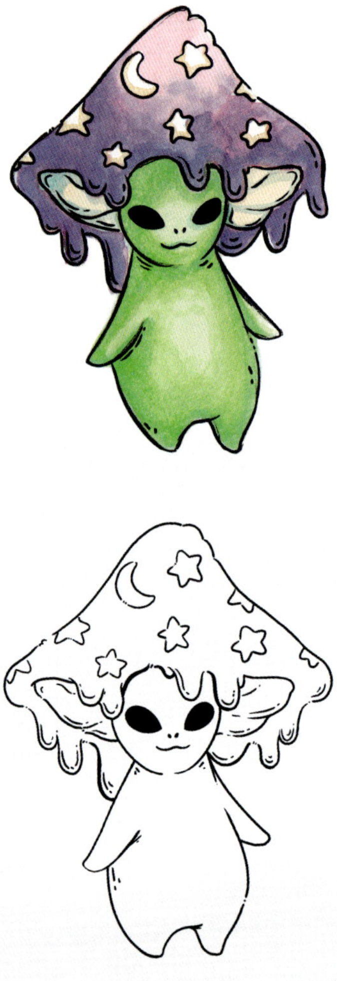

Alien Mushroom

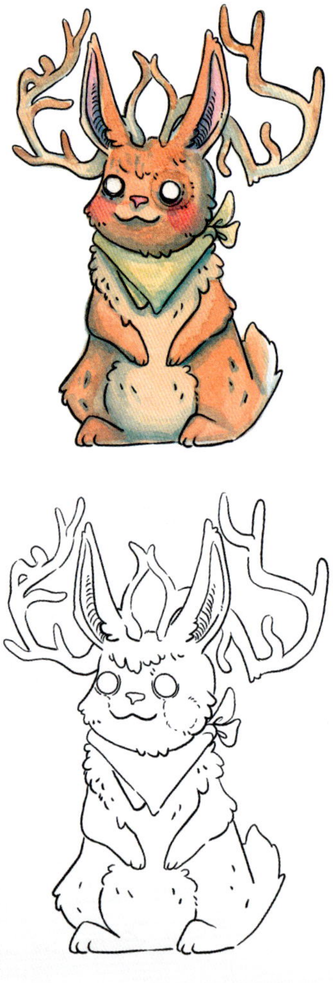

Jackalope

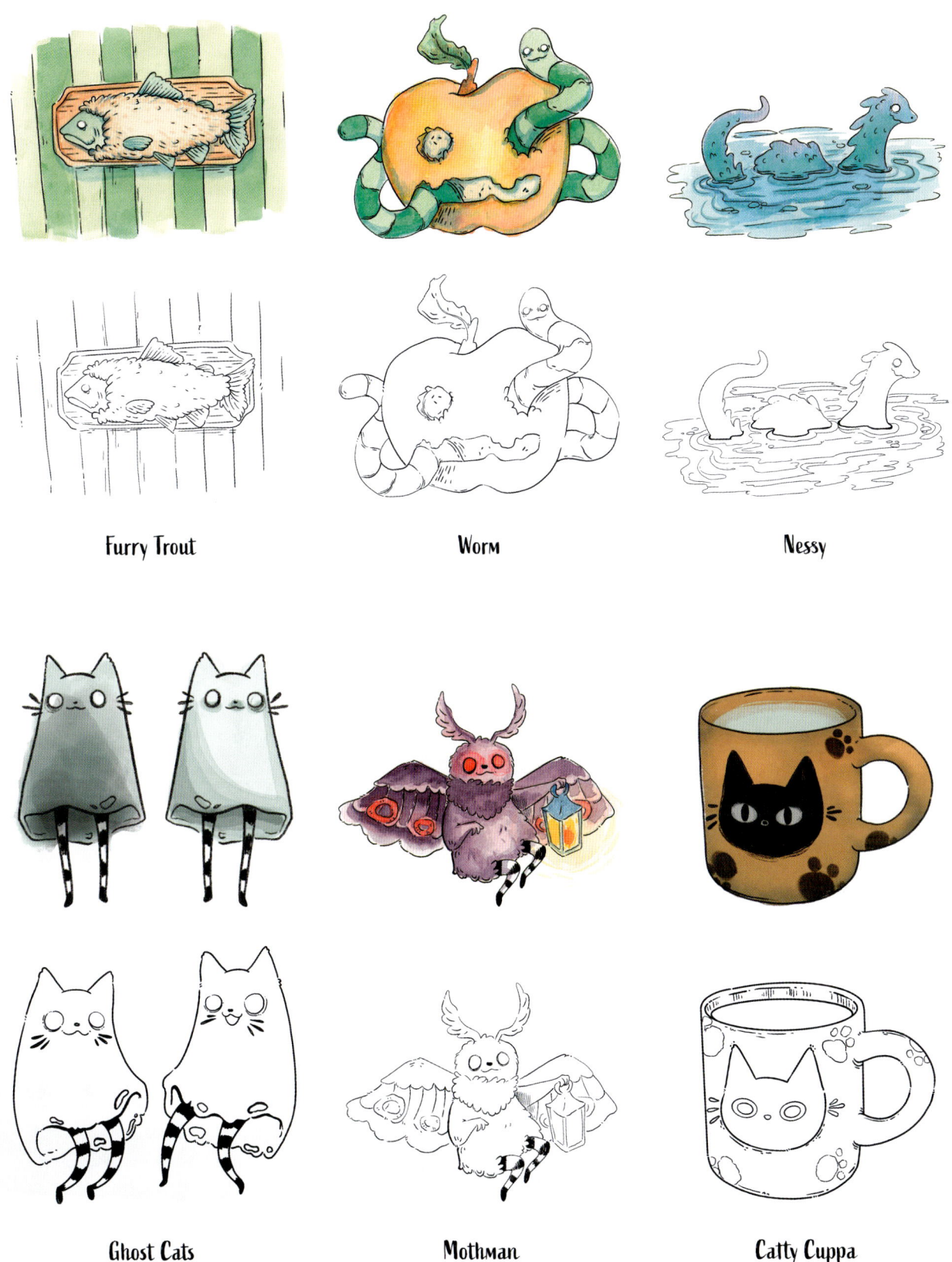

Furry Trout

Worm

Nessy

Ghost Cats

Mothman

Catty Cuppa

First Published in 2026 by Walter Foster Publishing, an imprint of The Quarto Group,
100 Cummings Center, Suite 265-D, Beverly, MA 01915, USA.
T (978) 282-9590 F (978) 283-2742

EEA Representation, WTS Tax d.o.o.,
Žanova ulica 3, 4000 Kranj, Slovenia.
www.wts-tax.si

Walter Foster Publishing titles are also available at discount for retail, wholesale, promotional, and bulk purchase. For details, contact the Special Sales Manager by email at specialsales@quarto.com or by mail at The Quarto Group, Attn: Special Sales Manager, 100 Cummings Center, Suite 265-D, Beverly, MA 01915, USA.

30 29 28 27 26 1 2 3 4 5

ISBN: 978-1-57715-686-4

Digital edition published in 2026
eISBN: 978-1-57715-687-1

Design and page layout: Marissa Mikolaities

Printed in Guangdong, China TT012026

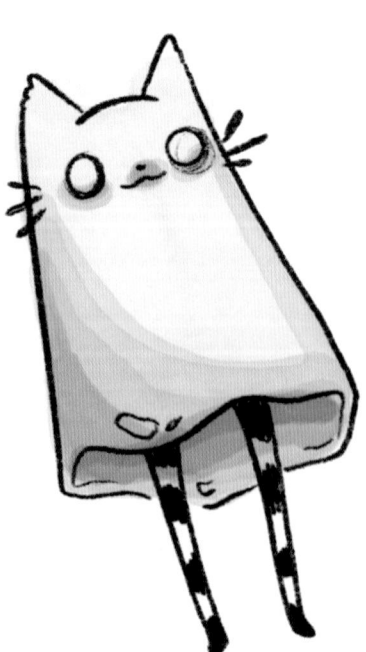